Christianity

Major World Religions Series

Donald K. Swearer, Editor

Christianity

BY HOWARD CLARK KEE, Ph.D.

Argus Communications
Niles, Illinois 60648

PHOTO CREDITS

BETTMANN ARCHIVE 95
BIBLIOTHEQUE NATIONALE, Paris 31
R. Darolle/SYGMA 46
Follett Publishing Co./KONRAN MEDIA cover: middle left
Weems Hutto cover: top left
R. V. Johnson/SHOSTAL ASSOCIATES 10
Howard Clark Kee 3, 14
V. Lefteroff/SHOSTAL ASSOCIATES cover: top right
Jean-Claude LeJeune 39
Ray Manley/SHOSTAL ASSOCIATES 51
NATIONAL PORTRAIT GALLERY, London 86
Courtesy New Covenant Magazine 106 (top and bottom)
Gerald Pillow/BRUCE COLEMAN INC. 82
Marc Rousseau/SHOSTAL ASSOCIATES 103
Kurt Scholz/SHOSTAL ASSOCIATES 54
SHOSTAL ASSOCIATES cover: bottom right; 23, 74
B. G. Silberstein/SHOSTAL ASSOCIATES 62
Q. Troisfontaines/SHOSTAL ASSOCIATES cover: bottom left

MAP AND COVER DESIGN
Gene Tarpey

Printed in the United States of America.

Argus Communications
7440 Natchez Avenue
Niles, Illinois 60648

International Standard Book Number 0-89505-021-8

Library of Congress Number 78-68769

0 9 8 7 6 5 4 3 2 1

Contents

Foreword

"The study of religion is the study of mankind." Religion touches the deepest feelings of the human heart and is part of every human society. In modern times religion has been studied by sociologists and anthropologists as a cultural institution. Psychologists see religion as an expression of an inner human need. Philosophers view it as a system of thought or doctrine. Historians consider religion a part of the intellectual and institutional development of a given era.

What is religion? Modern definitions range from "what man does in his solitude" to "an expression of collective identity," and from "man's experience of awe and fascination before a tremendous mystery" to "projective feelings of dependency." The scope of life that religion is identified with is so vast, and the assumptions about the nature of religion are so varied, that we may readily agree with those who say that the study of religion is the study of mankind.

Religion takes many forms, or perhaps it would be better to say that there are many aspects to religion. They include *belief* (e.g., the belief in a creator God), *ritual action* (e.g., making offerings to that God), *ethical action* (following God's law), the formation of *religious communities,* and the formulation of *creeds and doctrinal systems.*

Joachim Wach, a scholar of religion, has pictured religion in terms of religious experience which expresses itself in thought, action, and fellowship.[1] In this view religion is rooted in religious experience, and all other aspects of religion are expressions of that experience. For example, the Buddha's experience of the highest Truth (in Buddhism called *Nirvana*) led him to teach what he had experienced (known as *dharma*) and resulted in the formation of a monastic community (known as *sangha*).

It must be remembered that religions develop within particular historical and cultural traditions and not in a vacuum. This fact has several profound consequences for the study of religion. In the first place it means that religion can never be completely separated from particular historical and cultural traditions. For example, early Christian thought was deeply influenced by both Semitic and Greek traditions, and such central Christian celebrations as Christmas and Easter owe their form to pre-Christian European traditions.

---

[1]Joachim Wach, *The Comparative Study of Religions* (New York: Columbia University Press, 1958).

Furthermore, since a religion is subject to cultural and historical influences, its traditions are always developing relative to particular times and places. For example, the form of worship used in the Buddhist Churches of America (founded in the late nineteenth century) has as much or more in common with American Protestant worship services than with its traditional Japanese form. A religion, then, as part of a specific historical and cultural stream, changes through time and can be fully understood only in relationship to its historical and cultural forms. By way of generalization we might say that Christianity as a religion is only partially understood in terms of its central beliefs and that a fuller or more complete understanding demands a knowledge of its worldwide history and the influence of its various cultural traditions.

In the second place, since a religion develops within particular historical and cultural settings, it also influences its setting. In other words, there is a give-and-take relationship between a religion and its environment. For example, in traditional societies like medieval Europe, Christianity was the inspiration for much of the art and architecture. The same is true for traditional India, where Buddhism and Hinduism decisively affected artistic forms, or for traditional Persia with Islam. Of course, religion influences its environment in other than merely artistic realms. It has had profound effects on modes of behavior (ethics), conceptions of state (politics), forms of economic endeavor—indeed, on all aspects of life.

As a consequence of the pervasive influence of religion in so many aspects of human endeavor, students of religion and society have observed that in traditional societies religion was never isolated. That is, nothing within the given society was perceived as nonreligious or profane. Every meaningful act was seen as religious or sacred. Professor Robert Bellah of the University of California at Berkeley argues that in the West the split between the sacred and the profane or the differentiation of religion from other aspects of life did not really begin until about the time of the Protestant Reformation. He refers to that period as "early modern." Beginning with the early modern period onward to the present, religion has become more and more differentiated from Western culture. Thus, for example, it is no longer assumed that an American is a Protestant, whereas it is still largely assumed that a Thai is a Buddhist.

The question has been asked, "Can someone understand a religion in which he or she does not believe?" As the previous discussion of the nature of religion indicates, belief in the truth claims of a religious tradition is not a prerequisite for engaging in its study or even for understanding (i.e., making sense of) its beliefs and historical forms. The study of religion, however, does demand empathy and sympathy. To engage in the study of another religion for the purpose of proving that one's own is superior can only result in a distorted understanding of that tradition. Or, for that matter, if one who professes no religious belief approaches the study of religion with an inhibiting skepticism, then the beauty and richness of religion will be lost. For the believer, the study of another religious tradition should enhance his or her own faith-understanding; for the nonbeliever (i.e., agnostic), the study of religion should open up new dimensions of the human spirit.

The objective study of religion should be undertaken because of its inherent significance—because the understanding of cultures and societies, indeed, of humankind, is severely limited when such study is ignored. The study of our own tradition from its own particular creedal or denominational perspective is justifiably a part of our profession of faith. However, such study should not close us off from a sympathetic understanding of other religious traditions. Rather, such inquiry should open us to what we share in common with other religious persons, as well as to what is genuinely unique about our own religious beliefs and traditions.

Is the study of religion relevant today? The authors of this series believe the answer is a resounding "Yes!" The United States—indeed, the world—is in the midst of a profound transition period. The crisis confronting nations today cannot be reduced merely to economic inflation, political instability, and social upheaval. It is also one of values and convictions. The time has passed when we can ignore our crying need to reexamine such basic questions as who we are and where we are going—as individuals, as communities, and as a nation. The interest in Islam on the part of many American blacks, experimentation with various forms of Asian religions by the "Age of Aquarius" generation, and a resurgence of Christian piety on college campuses are particular responses to the crisis of identity through which we are currently passing.

The serious study of religion in the world today is not only legitimate but necessary. Today we need all of the forces we can muster in order to restore a sense of individual worth, moral community, and value direction. The sympathetic study of religion can contribute toward these goals and can be of assistance in helping us to recover an awareness of our common humanity too long overshadowed by our preoccupation with technological and material achievement. As has been popularly said, we have conquered outer space at the expense of inner space.

But why study non-Western religions? The reason is quite simple. We no longer live in relative isolation from the cultures of Asia and Africa. As a consequence the marketplace of ideas, values, and faiths is much broader than it used to be. We are in contact with them through popular books and the news media, but for the most part our acquaintance is superficial at best. Rather than looking at the religions imbedded in these cultures as quaint or bizarre—an unproductive enterprise—we should seek genuine understanding of them in the expectation of broadening, deepening, and hopefully clarifying our own personal identity and direction. The study of religion is, then, a twofold enterprise: engaging the religion(s) as it is, and engaging ourselves in the light of that religion.

The Argus Communications Major World Religions Series attempts to present the religious traditions of Judaism, Christianity, Islam, Hinduism, Buddhism, China, and Africa in their unity and variety. On the one hand, the authors interpret the traditions about which they are writing as a faith or a world view which instills the lives of their adherents with value, meaning, and direction. On the other hand, each volume attempts to analyze a particular religion in terms of its historical and cultural settings. This latter dimension means that the authors are interested in the present form of a religious tradition as well as its past development. How can Christianity or Judaism speak to the problems confronting Americans today? What are some of the new religions of Africa, and are they displacing traditional beliefs and world views? Can Maoism be considered the new religion of China? Is traditional Hinduism able to cope with India's social, economic, and political change? The answers to such questions form a legitimate and important part of the content of the series.

The author of each volume is a serious student and teacher of the tradition about which he or she is writing. Each has spent considerable time in countries where that religious tradition is part of the culture. Furthermore, as individuals, the authors are committed to the positive value the proper study of religion can have for students in these times of rapid social, political, and economic change. We hope that the series succeeds in its attempt to present the world's religions not as something "out there," a curiosity piece of times past, but as a subject of study relevant to the needs of our times.

Chapter 1

The World at the Time of Jesus' Birth

On the 26th of June, 363, the Roman emperor Julian lay dying of a stab wound in his abdomen. His military campaign against the Persians had failed, and he may have been stabbed by a disillusioned soldier or perhaps even on his own order. His attempt to discredit Christianity and to reestablish pagan worship as the religion of the Roman Empire had also failed. In fact, his efforts had made him look ridiculous even to his supporters. Legend has it that in Julian's final moments he caught some of his own blood in his hands and hurled it at the sun (which he worshipped as a god), crying out to Jesus in words that sound like the concession of a bitter, defeated politician: "Galilean, you won!"

But how did the Galilean win? What was it about Christianity that enabled it to triumph over its competitors in the early centuries A.D.? Actually, Julian's assessment of the situation was far too simple. No human institution or movement ever "wins" once and for all. In order to survive, every human enterprise must go through periods of adjustment, during which it adapts itself to new situations. It must reexamine its traditions, convictions, and institutions and provide new forms of expression and action so that they continue to have meaning for persons whose life and outlook are so different and so far removed from those among whom the movement first began.

In the political realm, the world's oldest written constitution—that of the United States—continues to function effectively only because built into it was the provision that through amendments, through interpretation by the courts, and through legislative action, the constitution could adjust to changing circumstances. It has thus been able to meet new needs and problems as they arose in the history of America. Similarly, the church would long since have vanished had it been a rigid, changeless institution founded on a fixed body of rules and beliefs. The story of Christianity, therefore, is a story of change, of transformation in response to new situations. Only thus could it have

1

continued to have meaning for millions of human beings for nearly two thousand years.

But before we examine how Christianity developed, let's look at the world—or that part known then as the "civilized world"—into which Christ was born.

A RELIGIOUS WORLD

When Paul the apostle was preaching the message about Jesus as God's agent for delivering the world from ignorance and evil, he reportedly flattered a crowd in the marketplace of Athens by telling them, "I perceive that in every way you are very religious" (Acts 17:22).[1] The problem that faced the early Christian propagandists was not a lack of interest in religious questions, since there were at that time plenty of gods and several wandering ascetics who claimed they brought the word of one God. The problem was to make persuasive the unique claims for Jesus as the answer to universal religious aspirations.

In the first century B.C. when the Romans began taking over the eastern half of the Mediterranean world, they encouraged religion as a unifying force. They did not seek to replace the temples and shrines of the Greek, Syrian, and Egyptian gods, or to hinder the Jews' worship of one God in the temple at Jerusalem. Rather they encouraged local shrines and, in many cases, Roman rulers reverently visited them.

The increased mobility of the population and the dominance of the Mediterranean world by a single military and political power meant that the gods, so to speak, traveled widely, as did their worshippers. Isis, honored primarily in Egypt as the mother-goddess, had shrines erected in her honor from eastern Syria to Spain. Aesclepius, the god of healing, was venerated not only at various places in Greece, but in Asia Minor and Rome. Healing gods in Phoenicia and Egypt came to be identified with him, so that seekers after the benefits of Aesclepius came from all geographic and ethnic quarters. At the same time, shrines devoted to the mystery gods, with promises of life after death

---

[1] This and all subsequent quotations from the Bible are from the Revised Standard Version.

The Temple of Apollo at Delphi is one of the remaining examples of religious shrines from the ancient Greek world.

(as at Eleusis, near Athens), were visited by many people. There were other divinities that revealed the future or offered solutions to vexing problems as at Delphi in Greece and Memphis in Egypt. Pilgrims assembled there from near and far.

What is shown by the popularity and extent of these shrines and oracles is that the basic human concerns, the threats to peaceful existence or even to life itself, were being dealt with through these divinities and oracles, with at least some degree of effectiveness.

Belief in magic in the first century was as intense as it was widespread. If one knew the proper techniques—whether secret words to be uttered, or herbs or secret substances to be applied, or certain rituals to be performed—the forces of evil could be overcome, and health and happiness achieved. Fortunately, ancient copies of magical documents have been preserved, as well as amulets and magical equipment, so that historians' knowledge of the practice of magic is extensive and detailed. Some of the rites performed at the shrines of deities were thought to guarantee rebirth and entrance into the realm of bliss beyond death. Ritual baths and the sacrifices to gods were thought to provide cleansing from guilt or pardon for disobedience to the will of the gods.

There were, of course, skeptics and rationalists who regarded the oracles as fake and dismissed the gods as childish illusions. But the fundamental human problems of sickness and death, of personal identity, of meaning in life, of the ever-present threat of disorder or the triumph of evil—these neither the skeptics nor magic nor anyone could cause to vanish.

AN AGE OF ANXIETY

The Roman Empire brought a political order to the Mediterranean world, but it also brought a feeling of dread and alienation. One of the prices paid for the Roman domination was that ethnic groups throughout the region lost all sense of being able to control their own destiny. Distant authorities and alien armies determined the course of their existence. At the same time greater freedom of movement of people throughout the empire resulted in chaotic cultural crosscurrents and conflicts. In the valley below the temple in Jerusalem a Roman racecourse was erected. In the delta of the Nile, Alexandria not only replaced Memphis as the center of Egyptian life but became the major center of Greek-style learning and research in the Roman world. Exposed to violent forms of change and suffering from culture shock, large numbers of people longed for a sense of reassurance, of identity and status. They sought it in one or both of the following ways: (1)

voluntary association with a group sharing a common commitment, and (2) dedication to a view of life as determined by the gods whose purposes would be achieved through a divinely endowed agent. As a result, secret societies flourished. Some of them were guilds (based on common occupation), but most were formed by groups of devotees of a particular divinity, such as Isis.

As long ago as the time of Hesiod, the earliest (eighth century B.C.) Greek poet, there had arisen a longing for a return of an earlier golden age of peace and prosperity which people assumed had once existed in far antiquity. The return of this age, they thought, would signal the final age of humankind. But now this nostalgia for a vanished Eden burst forth again. This prophetic yearning was given poetic expression by the Roman poet Virgil, who died in 19 B.C.:

> Now is come the last age . . . a new generation descends from heaven above . . . and a golden race springs up throughout the world. See how everything rejoices in the age that is at hand!

Others of a more prosaic type looked not for an Eden, but sought a remedy for the chaos of life in the philosophical concept of natural law. Assuming the existence of an unchanging order of nature, they said that everything took place in the universe according to inevitable laws and principles. What seemed to be evil or what caused human discomfort was nothing more, said the Stoics, than the chance collision of particles falling through space. Human responsibility, therefore, was to seek and discern and to live by the laws of nature, to display courage in the face of adversity, and to join in calm, reasonable associations with others of similar persuasion. This movement, which began in the fifth century B.C. under Zeno, took its name (Stoicism) from the public porticoes in Athens (the Stoa) where the Stoics instructed their pupils. They used the Stoa because they were too stingy to hire a private hall.

A CHANGING JEWISH WORLD

The Jews of this era were affected like everyone else by the cultural forces sweeping around them. They responded in a variety of ways to the invading Graeco-Roman culture. Some simply adopted it. They dressed like the Greeks and Romans and adopted their life-style. But others reacted in a violently negative way. One priestly family, which came to be known as the Maccabees (meaning "hammer"), led a revolt in 168 B.C. against Antiochus IV, the Greek king of Syria, who tried to force the Jews to take part in public ceremonies honoring him as a divine agent. But eventually even the Maccabean family fell increasingly under Greek influence. Finally their disgusted, pious subjects were relieved when the Romans came in 63 B.C. and deposed the Jewish royal line.

Most Jews were influenced by the culture in more subtle ways. The Pharisees, for example, tried to avoid contamination with the new cultures by setting up the Law of Moses as the ultimate authority, attributing to it an eternal existence not unlike that of Stoic natural law. The Pharisees insisted on living in conformity to their law, as the Stoics did to the laws of nature.

Even with these examples of the Maccabees and the Pharisees, many Jews became lax in their faith. In spite of their Bible's prohibition against images of living things, wealthy Jews decorated their houses, their tombs, and even their synagogues with Greek-style sculpture and mosaics, even to the point of displaying the signs of the zodiac and portraying their God, Yahweh, as the sun-god on the synagogue pavements.

Other Jews became utterly disillusioned about their nation, its leadership, and its future. Accordingly, they withdrew completely from urban or village life and retreated to monastic settlements on the edge of the desert. We know of one such group near Alexandria. The structures and library of another have been found in recent years west of where the Jordan River empties into the Dead Sea. These people, however, did share a conviction that was prevalent throughout that part of the world: only divine intervention could restore the world to the peace and beauty it had known earlier. The Jews, unlike the Greeks and Romans, believed in only one God, Yahweh. He would continue to reveal His purposes through chosen spokesmen within the Jewish group. Some of them were granted prophetic visions and oracles, and others were enabled, by God, to interpret ancient scriptures of Judaism in such a way as to disclose God's purpose. But they believed that God had chosen to hide His purpose from all but the elect community, the chosen people, who were the Jews.

One place where all these conflicting influences were strongly felt at this time was the district of Galilee, in northern Palestine. There Jews lived side by side with Gentiles. In the cities around the Sea of Galilee, conservative interpreters of the Law of Moses had to compete for public attention with the hedonism of Roman life and the pronouncements of Stoic philosophers. Not far away in an obscure village in the hills, no doubt aware of all this confusion, lived a carpenter's son, known as Jesus of Nazareth.

Chapter 2

The Beginning of Christianity

Our knowledge about Jesus is limited largely to the information provided by the four little writings, called gospels, that stand at the beginning of the collection now known as the New Testament. Although these works are all anonymous, ancient tradition has linked them with followers of Jesus or of their associates: Matthew, a disciple; Mark, a companion of Peter; Luke, an associate of Paul; and John, a disciple. The gospels, which were probably written in the last third of the first century, embody oral and written traditions about Jesus preserved in various segments of the early church.

JESUS' EARLY LIFE

In Luke 4:16–30, there is an idealized description of Jesus leading his fellow townspeople in worship in the synagogue at Nazareth. This is the first appearance he makes in public life. The other gospels simply depict him as returning from his experiences with John the Baptist in the Jordan Valley and launching a preaching crusade, in which he announced that God's kingdom (or New Age) was drawing near. What would have qualified him to preach in this way? What authority did he have for announcing that the new era promised by prophets of Israel was about to appear? Unfortunately, there is no reliable information about his childhood or his training. Matthew and Luke have accounts of miraculous events accompanying his birth in Bethlehem (Matthew 1:18–2:23; Luke 1:26–2:20), but they do not agree on why Jesus' family was there. (In Matthew, they lived there. In Luke, they had to go there for census purposes.) Nor do they agree on several other details.

Prominent in the narratives of Matthew and Luke is the mention of the fulfillment of scripture, by which each writer wants to prove to his readers that what happened in connection with Jesus was the operation of a divine plan: Jesus was the Messiah whose coming had so often been announced. These two gospel writers turn to different scriptures and, accordingly, present different evidence for their claims in Jesus' behalf. One might expect that pagan sources of the time would supplement or correct the information about Jesus provided by the gospels. But from nonbiblical sources, we have only the acknowledgment that Jesus lived, that he was crucified, and that a powerful movement started in his name. Some historians have assumed that he was reared like other Palestinian Jewish boys of his time. But even if he were, that does not help to explain why he turned out so differently.

We are on much surer ground historically when we begin where the gospel accounts converge—with the launching of Jesus' career as preacher and healer following his time with John the Baptist (Mark 1, Matthew 3, Luke 3, John 1).

THE INFLUENCE OF JOHN THE BAPTIST

John is a vivid example of the prophetic messengers whose voices were being heard in Palestine at the time of Jesus. He seems to have modeled his dress and his manner of life from the ancient prophet Elijah. Clad in animal skins and living austerely, John echoed the words of the prophets: God would send Elijah back to earth before the end of the present age in order to call humankind to repentance and to prepare for God's final judgment of the human race.

John was believed to be God's messenger who would precede His final action in establishing the New Age (Mark 1:2; cf. Malachi 3:1). Men and women could prepare for the judgment and the Age to Come by acknowledging their sin and giving public testimony of their repentance by accepting baptism in the muddy waters of the Jordan River.

Ages before, it was believed, God had brought together in the desert of Sinai diverse tribes and entered into a mutual commitment, or covenant, with them. He would be their God and they would be His obedient people. So, just as ancient Israel had passed through the Jordan on its historic journey from Egypt to the Promised Land, where they would become God's people, so John's penitents would move through the Jordan waters in order to emerge as members of God's New Covenant people.

At a settlement near the Dead Sea it was believed that one could not enter the community of the New Covenant unless one withdrew totally from society. But John seems to have understood the prophecy of Jeremiah about the New Covenant (Jeremiah 31:31–34) to mean that it required a change of heart rather than racial or ritual purity. Additional information in Luke 3:10–14 implies that in his redefined covenant he included persons of different occupations and backgrounds. Therefore, according to John, a repentant new people of God was taking shape on the edge of the Judean desert at the hands of John the Baptist. Among those attracted by this undertaking and by its promise was Jesus of Nazareth (Mark 1:9). From John, Jesus received baptism, and with it a commitment to prepare for God's New Age.

According to three of the gospels, Jesus' association with John was brief but it had a powerful effect. They all report that Jesus was divinely commissioned at the moment of baptism. This was followed by a period of self-examination and testing in the wilderness, just as other leaders of ancient Israel—Moses and Elijah—had undergone periods of struggle alone in the desert in preparation for service. John's gospel, however, suggests that the relationship with John the Baptist continued much longer, with Jesus carrying on baptismal activity on his own (John 3:22). From John he acquired the inner core of his own disciples (John 1:37, 40). Perhaps it was out of respect for John that Jesus did not launch his own mission until the Baptist was taken off the scene and imprisoned (Mark 1:14).

JESUS' MESSAGE

In any case, Jesus' message and strategy were significantly different from those of John. They both shared the belief that God was about to establish His rule (or kingdom) on earth, and that in preparation for it, he was summoning together a new people. But contrary to John, who preached doom and judgment, Jesus emphasized the joy, the good news that God was about to establish heaven on earth. The English word *gospel* comes from the Greek term *evangelion* (meaning "good news"), from which is derived *evangel* and related words. Jesus' message of good news about what God intended to do was matched by the good deeds which he performed among his hearers. Like many of his contemporaries, Jesus is depicted as believing that sickness is linked with sin and with the power of evil spirits. Accordingly, he appears in the gospel narratives announcing that God has authorized him to subjugate the evil spirits and to announce the forgiveness of sins in preparation for the New Age.

The stricter among Jesus' fellow Jews would have been reluctant to associate with the demon-possessed persons and those with such illnesses as leprosy (or whatever gross skin disease is meant in Mark 1:40). Most Jews would have refused to accept the hospitality of non-Jews, such as the Roman officer who asked Jesus to heal his servant (Luke 7:1–10). Nor would they have associated with Gentiles and renegade Jews, as Jesus is represented doing in various accounts in the gospels. For a Jew concerned about ceremonial purity, the visit to Gerasa (Mark 5) would have been unthinkable on several counts: the district was strongly influenced by Greek culture and was the home of

several pagan philosophers; Jesus' convert was a demoniac who lived in tombs, where contact with dead bodies made Jews ritually unclean; there were also herds of pigs wandering about. Why did Jesus associate with unclean persons, like the Syro-Phoenician woman, whose daughter he healed?

The answer is, at least in part, that his behavior was not in the Jewish tradition. The closest analogy we have to the methods and strategy of Jesus and his followers is the itinerant philosophers and miracle workers whose scorn of such basic social institutions as family and job is reported in ancient sources. These sources were well known during the early Roman period. Certainly Jesus called his followers to leave their means of livelihood (Mark 1:16–20) and to abandon their wives and families (Mark 10:29). Unlike the wandering philosophers, however, the motive for the break with domestic and economic stability was not scorn. It was a sense of urgency born of the belief that God was bringing the whole world order to a consummation when it would be replaced by a new society. The fact that Jesus seems never to have married in a society where marriage was the accepted pattern of life suggests that he shared the view that the New Age was so near at hand that all other human obligations must be laid aside.

JESUS' REINTERPRETATION OF THE LAW

Jesus did not reject the Law of Moses, according to gospel accounts, but gave it a new set of interpretations that had radical consequences for his followers, and served to arouse the Jewish authorities' hostility toward him. The contrast between his understanding of God's will as expressed in the Law and that of his Jewish contemporaries is shown in bold relief in the series of contrasts found in the Sermon on the Mount (actually a collection of sayings of Jesus in Matthew 5–7): "You have heard that it was said to the men of old [that is, by the official interpreters of the Law], but I say to you . . ." (Matthew 5:21, 27, 31, 33, 38, 43).

Jesus in many cases intensified the demands of the Law. For example, there were some grounds for divorce at the time, but Jesus, according to Mark 10:11, would not permit it at all. According to

The Jordan River, where John baptized Jesus.

11

Matthew 5:31, it was allowed only when adultery had been committed. But adultery was defined as not only overt acts of sexual promiscuity but even lustful looks.

Still more stringent are the teachings which prohibit oaths under any circumstances (Matthew 5:34), and which call for responding to the evil deeds of others with kindness (Matthew 5:38–42). Enemies are to be loved, not hated. The basis of the moral appeal is not the specifics of the Law but the loving, gracious nature of God himself (Matthew 5:45). Wealth and abundance are not to be regarded as signs of divine favor; rather the poor, the deprived, and the hated are those for whom God has a reward when His rule is established on earth (Luke 6:20–23).

In other cases of the Law, however, specific legal requirements were set aside in the face of basic human needs. For example, preparing food on the sabbath or healing the sick on that sacred day—forbidden in a strict interpretation of the Law—were actions defended by Jesus according to Mark 2:23–3:6. The Jewish tradition about fasting was also abandoned in view of the joyous new situation that had come with the announcement of the coming of God's rule (Mark 2:18–22). It was these abrogations of the specific requirements of the Law in favor of human need that led the religious opposition to form a coalition to destroy Jesus (Mark 3:6).

GROWING OPPOSITION

The religious and political authorities of Palestine could easily find common cause against Jesus. He had violated the Law and encouraged others to do so. Inevitably he was regarded by the religious establishment as arrogant and deserving of the severest punishment. Roman policy allowed religious officials to mete out justice when sacred laws of a particular segment of the population were broken. The Jewish mode of execution for those found guilty of capital crimes was stoning. The culprit was hurled over a precipice, and the crowd then threw down large rocks to crush him to death. At the same time the mound of stones over the body prevented its polluting the vicinity.

But Jesus had done more, in Jewish eyes, than break the Law. He reportedly claimed that God would vindicate him even if his opponents killed him. At the dawn of the New Age, Jesus said his enemies would be made to suffer (Mark 8:38) and his friends would be rewarded (Mark 9:1). Even before that, he predicted the great Temple of Jerusalem—an enormous and splendid structure built by the non-Jewish king of the Jews, Herod the Great—would be destroyed (Mark 13:2). He had warned of this when he entered the temple courts and protested publicly that the place of worship had become a busy, commerical enterprise and, indeed, a "den of robbers" (Mark 11:17).

Jesus, according to the oldest gospel, Mark, never precisely claimed to be the Messiah (God's anointed agent to establish His rule). But he did allow his disciples to designate him as such (in Greek, *Christ;* Mark 8:29). And he rode into Jerusalem on a donkey, apparently in conscious enactment of the prophecy of Zechariah 9, which predicted that Israel's king would enter the city mounted on a lowly ass. Faced with the direct question "Are you the Christ?" in the hearing before the Jewish religious council, he gave only the ambiguous response, "So you say" (Matthew 26:64). Reports of these kingly claims—whether Jesus had made them in his own behalf or not—understandably aroused the fears of the local Roman governor, Pontius Pilate. Did he have a revolution of Jewish nationalists on his hands? He seemed to believe that Jesus was leading an insurrectionist movement. Pilate was able to capture Jesus through the connivance of one of Jesus' own followers. The traitor Judas led the Roman soldiers to the place outside the city walls of Jerusalem where Jesus and his disciples were spending the night. There Jesus was seized. After a hearing before the religious authorities, Pilate condemned Jesus to death. He was crucified, a peculiarly Roman mode of execution reserved for non-Roman citizens. The inscription above the cross announced that Jesus had claimed to be king of the Jews—a threat to the authority of the Roman government, and hence worthy of death.

DEATH AND RESURRECTION

The only clue we have as to how Jesus understood his own role in God's purpose is what he said at his final meal with his followers. This covenant-type meal seems to have resembled the ceremonial meal of the Dead Sea community, in which the members celebrated their common purpose as God's obedient people and their belief that God would vindicate them in the future. After distributing the bread and wine, Jesus is reported to have said: "This is my blood of the covenant which is poured out for many. Truly I say to you, I shall not drink of the fruit of the vine until that day when I drink it new in the Kingdom of God" (Mark 14:24–25). This implies that Jesus knew he was going to be put to death. It also implies that he saw his death ("blood . . . poured out") not as a defeat, but as a symbol and example of the suffering that God's people must endure until that time when God vindicates His own.

Initially the reaction of Jesus' followers to his gruesome death was one of terror and disillusionment. All but a few women fled. Peter, the

chief spokesman of the disciples, denied even knowing Jesus. Within a few days, however, the situation was transformed. His followers claimed that they had seen him alive and that he had commissioned them to carry on with the mission of calling men and women to share in the community of the New Age, when God's kingdom was sovereign "on earth as it is in heaven" (Matthew 6:10).

According to the earliest testimony (Paul's letter, I Corinthians 15:5), it was Peter, the vehement denier of Jesus, who first saw him risen from the dead. Paul reports that this experience was followed by an appearance to the twelve disciples, and later to hundreds of others. Among those were James—Jesus' brother, who seems to have shared the family view that Jesus was a madman (Mark 3:21, 31)—and even Paul himself, who had been a persecutor of the followers of Jesus (I Corinthians 15:8–9). Later tradition describes these visions of the risen Lord in detail, including the presence of angels, voices from heaven, and the claim that Jesus' body was physical, which was attested by his being touched, by his displaying his wounds, and by his eating food.

Historical investigation of the belief that God raised Jesus from the dead is necessarily limited to the effects brought about by this conviction. The cause that gave rise to the resurrection faith is simply not subject to historical analysis.

Of all those listed by Paul as having seen "the Lord," as the early Christians uniformly called Jesus after the emergence of the resurrection faith (I Corinthians 9:1; John 21:21; Luke 24:34), only Paul provided an account of the impact which this experience had upon him. Legends and late traditions recount where other disciples went to spread the message about Jesus as the Lord and bringer of God's kingdom. For example, Peter is linked with Rome, John with Ephesus, Mark with Alexandria, Thomas with India. But there is no certain evidence. What is certain is that they traveled about. Paul describes meeting Peter in the church at Antioch in Syria (Galatians 2:11). It was here that Paul called Peter by his Semitic nickname—*Kepha*, or Cephas, meaning "the Rock." The fact that the original disciples acknowledged Paul's conversion in spite of their differences with him on such matters as Gentile Christian observance of dietary laws (Galatians 2:12–14) strongly suggests that his vision of the resurrected Lord matched well with their own.

A model of Jerusalem at the time of Herod.

Chapter 3

Early Church Development

The Christian church (in Greek, *ekklesia,* meaning "assembly" or "community") spread rapidly following the rise of the resurrection faith. The Acts of the Apostles, which was written probably toward the end of the first century, depicts the spread of Christianity in an orderly series of widening circles: "In Jerusalem and all Judea and Samaria and to the end of the earth" (Acts 1:8). The narrative of Acts describes the process as moving by deliberate decisions and divine revelations from Jerusalem northward to Samaria, westward to Caesarea on the Mediterranean coast, northeastward to Damascus, and from there to Antioch, Asia Minor, the Greek cities around the Aegean Sea, and finally to Rome.

There are hints in Acts, however, that there were Christian communities elsewhere throughout the empire before Paul journeyed westward to Rome. Paul's associates in Corinth included a Jewish couple who had fled from Rome, where Jews, including Jewish Christians, were undergoing imperial persecution (Acts 18:1–4). In Ephesus, a convert from Alexandria appears to assist Paul in his work of evangelism (Acts 18:24). In fact, by the time of Paul's conversion, there was already a church in Damascus. It must have been flourishing even then or Paul would not have felt obligated to destroy it (Galatians 1:13–17).

We learn from Acts of evangelistic activity in Ethiopia, in Cyprus, and in northern Greece (Macedonia). By Paul's own account (Romans 15:19, 23), there was no unevangelized region in the entire quadrant of the Mediterranean lands from Jerusalem north and westward to the Adriatic coast. Roman sources (the letters of Pliny, governor of Bithynia, a district in what is now Turkey) reveal that the church was a highly visible enterprise in eastern Asia Minor early in the second century—so much so that the governor had to ask the emperor for guidelines in dealing with it. Eusebius, advisor to Emperor Constantine in the fourth century, records traditions about the journeys and activities of the disciples and their associates reaching as far as India.

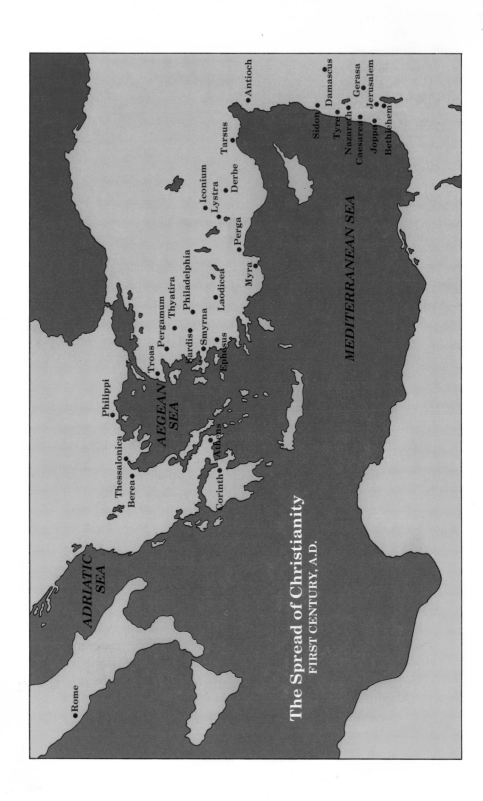

The Spread of Christianity
FIRST CENTURY, A.D.

Rome

ADRIATIC SEA

Philippi

Thessalonica
Berea

Corinth
Athens

AEGEAN SEA

Troas

Pergamum
Thyatira
Sardis
Smyrna
Ephesus

Philadelphia

Laodicea

Myra

Perga

Derbe

Lystra
Iconium

Tarsus

Antioch

MEDITERRANEAN SEA

Sidon
Damascus
Tyre
Nazareth
Caesarea
Gerasa
Jerusalem
Joppa
Bethlehem

Yet none of these sources adds significantly or reliably to our knowledge of the geographical spread of Christianity in the first century of its existence. But there are two lines of evidence, other than geographical, that are of importance in tracing the development of early Christianity and the church structure.

APOSTOLIC AUTHORITY
AND CHURCH LEADERSHIP

The first line of evidence is the evolving concept of apostolic authority. Paul implies that the prime qualification for being an apostle is to have seen Jesus risen from the dead (I Corinthians 9:1). Although he mentions hundreds who had "seen the Lord," we cannot assume that these witnesses to the resurrection were apostles. But we can assume that all twelve apostles were resurrection witnesses. As the term *apostle* suggests in its Greek original *(apostolos,* from the verb *apostello,* meaning "to send" or "to commission"), the apostles believed themselves to have been commissioned and empowered by the risen Jesus to carry forward the word which he had begun during his historic ministry. The exercise of apostolic authority in the churches apparently included rendering solemn judgments on members of the community whose behavior was contrary to what the apostles judged appropriate for Christians (I Corinthians 5:1–5). The seeds of the later practice of excommunication are evident in the solemn display of apostolic judicial power. The power of the later bishops, and indeed the pope himself, derives from this early power given to the original apostles.

Later books of the New Testament, written in the name of Paul but probably penned by his followers or successors (just as Plato wrote in the name of his teacher, Socrates), give evidence that the church began to develop levels of leadership. In I Timothy, the various offices in the church are described: bishops, deacons, "widows" (nuns?), elders, each of whom had specified qualifications to meet and duties to perform. Inevitably, any human institution must develop a division of labor and a structure for decision making. This is what can be seen emerging in the later New Testament writings. Linked with this is the authority that clings to Paul's name and to the other apostles, as well as the power of their lives as examples and of their writings as authoritative statements for the church (II Timothy 3:10–16; II Peter 3:14–16). There is indeed a document from the early second century called *The Teachings of the Twelve Apostles* (in Greek, *Didache),* which offers detailed instructions on such practical problems as to how the Communion, or *Eucharist* (Greek for "giving thanks"), is to be celebrated, how itinerant prophets who may visit the church are to be evaluated, and how disputes are to be settled between bishops and deacons.

The second-century letters of Ignatius, sent to various churches in Asia Minor, assume that there is a single bishop who exercises authority over the church in each city and whose word is to be obeyed. This contrasts with the earlier I Timothy, where the word *bishops* (meaning "overseers") is used in the plural. It is also so used in Paul's letter to the Philippians (1:1). What is evident in these second-century writings, and especially in the letter of Clement of Rome to the church in Corinth, is that norms for behavior and for worship, as well as lines of authority, were slowly evolving. These were necessary if the churches were to function effectively. It is apparent in this literature that the church had moved to an era in which its leadership looked back with veneration to the first generation of apostles. As Ignatius wrote to the people of Smyrna:

> You should all follow the bishop as Jesus Christ did the Father. Follow, too, the presbytery (Council of Elders) as you would the apostles; and respect the deacons as you would God's law. Nobody must do anything that has to do with the church without the bishop's approval.

These leaders of the church in the second century did not abandon the belief that the present age was coming to an end and that they must be ready to stand before God in the Day of Judgment. But the sense of imminence had waned, and there was far more attention paid to order and stability, to right teaching, and to the exercise of authority than was the case among the first generation of Christians.

NEW TESTAMENT WRITINGS

The second line of evidence of the changing circumstances of the church as it spread into the wider Gentile world can be seen in the New Testament writings. They display a wide range of social and cultural conditions into which the Christian tradition was introduced and appropriated.

Matthew

The document which stands closer to the outlook of rabbinic Judaism than Paul or any other New Testament writer is the Gospel of Matthew. Although the pattern is incompletely carried out, the writer has arranged his material in five main sections (preceded by the birth stories and followed by the account of the trial and execution), perhaps in conscious imitation of the Five Books of Moses (Genesis, Exodus, Leviticus, Numbers, Deuteronomy). The highlight of the book comes in a set of instructions offered on a mountain in Galilee, just as Moses conveyed the will of God to Israel from a mountain slope in Sinai. Matthew alone reports that Jesus insisted that all of the law be fulfilled, all its claims accomplished (Matthew 5:17–18). More importantly, the church is implicitly defined as the true Israel, among whom the promises of God have been and are being fulfilled, and whose righteous mode of life is more stringent than that of the Pharisees. The leadership of historic Israel is condemned in the bitterest terms ("His blood be on us and on our children," the Jewish people cry out in Matthew 27:25); yet the establishment of God's rule will find Jesus and his followers in leadership roles over "the twelve tribes of Israel" (Matthew 19:28). Although "Israel" is not thought of by Matthew as an ethnic entity—disciples are to be drawn from all nations (Matthew 28:19)—it is a reconstitution of the covenant people of God, living by the regulation laid down in scripture as reinterpreted by Jesus, the Shepherd of the New Israel (Matthew 10:6; 15:24).

Mark

Mark's gospel was the first to be written and may have been completed before the fall of Jerusalem to the Romans in A.D. 66–70. In any event, it expects a speedy end to the present age, since some of Jesus' followers will be alive to witness it (Mark 9:1). It regards the Christian community as an elect group to whom the secret of the coming rule of God has been disclosed (Mark 4:11–12), while outsiders can only regard the Christian message as meaningless riddles. Although the sayings of Jesus furnish guidelines by which the church can be obedient to God's will, there is in Mark no provision for organizational structure or for fixed ethical norms. Apparently Mark felt that concern for money and economic stability would only divert energy from the more important task of proclaiming that the kingdom of God has drawn near (Mark 1:15).

John

Under the influence of Jewish speculation about the wisdom of God as the creator and guide of the world, the writer of the Gospel of John represents Jesus as the incarnation of God's purpose, or Word (in Greek, *logos*). His teachings and actions constitute an elaborate revelation of God to God's chosen people. As in Mark, outsiders are not able to grasp the truth about Jesus. But unlike Mark, the community in

John has little concern for the future kingdom; rather, the kingdom is a spiritual sphere into which men and women may enter now by faith ("Except a man is born again, he cannot enter the kingdom of God"— John 3:3). According to John, Jesus does not merely disclose the truth about God; he also embodies it. He *is* the water that refreshes human life, the bread that sustains it, the shepherd that guides it, the vine that nurtures it, the light and truth that illumine it. All of Jesus' miracles are symbolic acts that reinforce his power as the mystical agent ("You in me and I in you"—John 15) by which the faithful are joined to God and their lives thereby renewed. Sight to the blind, water changed into wine, bread from heaven, restoration of the dead to life are all metaphors of spiritual transformation that is experienced within the Christian community. Scholars have noted that John's language and religious style have links not only with Jewish speculation about wisdom, but also with the worship of Isis, whose shrines often enclose pronouncements of her virtues that begin with "I am the one who . . . ." Throughout John's gospel, Jesus reportedly describes himself as the "I am" who brings light, truth, and life to his people. All three divine agents (wisdom, Isis, and the Logos of John) are depicted as the instruments by which the world was created (John 1:10–12) and by which humanity may know God (John 8:12; 14:6).

Luke and Acts

Surely one of the most significant documents for the subsequent history of the church, however, is the two-volume work divided in the New Testament into the Gospel of Luke and the Acts of the Apostles. As the opening paragraphs of each show, they were originally parts of a unified work in which the author traced the progress of God's purpose in the world from the birth of Jesus to the arrival of the gospel in Rome, in the person of Paul. Throughout both volumes the author stresses the fact that the coming of Jesus was intended to benefit all humanity. He alone includes the quotation at the outset of Jesus' public ministry, "And all flesh [that is, all humanity] shall see the salvation of our God" (Luke 3:6). Luke alone reports such traditions about Jesus as the parable of the good Samaritan. He places unique emphasis on God's initiative in seeking out the "lost." Of all the residents of Jericho,

An illumination of Jesus feeding the multitude, from the Book of Hours of the Duke of Berry.

Etait iherusa gaudete am letaca qui
lem et conue tristicia fuistis ut eultetis
nim facite et facemum ab uberibus
omnes qui diligitis eam consolaconis uir. ps.

Jesus befriends Zacchaeus, a tax collector and social outcast. Luke groups the parable of the lost coin and the parable of the lost son with the parable of the lost sheep to show that it is the despised in society who are the beneficiaries of grace. Jesus, the bearer of light, was to illumine "all peoples, a light for revelation to the Gentiles," and to come "for the glory of thy people Israel" (Luke 2:31–32).

Luke's outreach to the Gentile world is both more pervasive and more subtle than these direct evidences might suggest. The literary features of his twofold writing include standard styles and strategies that would be familiar to readers of secular historians of Luke's time. The formal introductions to both volumes embody a style well known and widely used among Hellenistic historians. The composition of extended speeches, placed on the lips of the major characters in his narrative, is also a device in common use among writers of his epoch. The extended, vivid narrative detail, as in the long account of the storm and shipwreck on Paul's journey to Rome (Acts 27–28), displays a literary character that would have had a wide appeal among the reading public in the Roman world of his time. In short, Luke wants even those who do not share his Christian convictions to take him seriously as an author.

More directly appealing to a neutral reader, Luke reports that the early Christians—from Jesus to Paul—were often brought before the civil authorities but that in not a single instance were the political rulers able to make a charge stick against them. Even the final encounter of Paul with the Roman officials is left up in the air by Luke. Paul is under house arrest, but no accusation against him can be made to stick. The implication of all this is clear: Christianity is not a subversive movement.

The Christians, Luke implies, are articulate persons who in rather elegant form can offer defenses for their views. They can score points in debates with Jewish interpreters of the Law. They can meet Greek philosophers on their own ground, in Athens and elsewhere, and demonstrate the basic compatibility of much of what both groups believe. The universality of the knowledge of God is affirmed by Peter in Caesarea (Acts 10:34) and by Paul on the Areopagus, a small hill which served as the public debating center in Athens (Acts 17:27–28). In his own letters Paul acknowledged that, to the Greeks, his message would sound like foolishness (I Corinthians 1:23). But for the author of Acts, Paul was a man who could shape his message in ways that appealed to thoughtful pagans. As the narrative of the address on the Areopagus shows, Paul's gospel was not to be dismissed out of hand before he had been granted a fair hearing. As Luke saw it, the issue was not Paul's effectiveness in conveying his message to the Greeks but the message itself, the central distinctive claim of the Christians: God had raised Jesus from the dead (Acts 17:31–32). There was no dodging the intellectual problem of the resurrection, but for Luke there was every reason to establish as much common ground as possible before meeting that issue head-on.

The position of Paul awaiting trial in Rome became a symbol, perhaps unconsciously used by Luke, for the fate of Christianity at the hands of the imperial authorities. Acts portrays Paul as expecting his execution at the hands of the authorities (20:25), although the writer represents him as thinking that it will take place in Jerusalem rather than in Rome. This literary strategem of Luke's embodies a profound—one might say prophetic—historical insight. From this point on, the conflict that Christianity must face was not with Judaism but with the imperial power. After the fall of Jerusalem in A.D. 70, Judaism became a religious rather than a national entity. Until the establishment of the state of Israel in the twentieth century, Jews never had sustained political independence from the time of the Roman takeover of the city of Jerusalem in 63 B.C. A second violent but fruitless attempt at insurrection in the first third of the second century resulted in the expulsion of the Jews from Jerusalem and the transformation of the city into a pagan provincial center, with a Roman temple replacing the shrine of Yahweh on the temple mount. The major surviving element of the Jews, the Pharisaic rabbis, became nonpolitical, devoting themselves rather to the interpretation of the Law of Moses and the resultant maintenance of purity of the Jewish community on ritual and moral grounds. Bitter attacks were launched by Jews and Christians against each other, but Jerusalem was never again a threat to the Christian movement. The opponent of the church was now Rome itself.

CHRISTIAN PERSECUTION

Paul expected to be martyred (Philippians 2:17) and he was quite right. He was killed as were large numbers of other Christians. He rejoiced that during his imprisonment he did have the opportunity to preach to the guard in whose custody he had been placed (Philippians 1:12–13), although he longed for release from prison so that he might resume his work (Philippians 1:24). Yet in life or death, the model of his deportment was Jesus who had been obedient unto death (Philippians 2:8) and had been exalted by God.

Widespread martyrdom of Christians began in Rome, presumably during the later years of Nero's reign (54–68). Tradition, preserved in

Eusebius' *Ecclesiastical History* (Bk. II.25), holds that in his madness Nero began slaughtering Christians in Rome. Paul, a Roman citizen, was beheaded and Peter, a noncitizen, was crucified. Great churches honoring those apostolic martyrs were erected early in Rome and in altered form still stand as monuments to their faith and courage.

Domitian, who reigned as emperor from 81 to 96, halted the persecution and banishment of Christians, but he too was slightly mad. He executed his cousins Flavius Clemens and Domitilla, most likely because they converted to Christianity. He insisted that he be addressed as "Lord and God," which caused anxieties among the Christians.

During the reign of Trajan (98–117), attacks on the Christians erupted once more. Although Rome had always been tolerant toward local cults and divinities, the Christians' refusal to take part in any ceremonies or to offer sacrifices to the gods was viewed by the Roman pagans as atheism. Whenever a catastrophe occurred, such as a flood or a famine, it was blamed on the Christians. It was thought that by spurning the gods, the Christians had made them angry. Earlier, Nero had blamed the fires that swept Rome on the Christians, who were convenient scapegoats.

As the Christian movement flourished, attendance at local temples fell off, with a resultant slump in tourist traffic. There were fewer purchases of meat for the temple sacrifices. The economy was hurting. Accordingly, Trajan instructed Pliny, governor of Bithynia, to execute those who persisted in their Christianity and refused to offer sacrifices to the gods. He did warn the governor, however, not to seek out Christians or to invite informers to identify them, which showed a certain restraint.

It is quite possible that the Roman authorities in Syria wanted to make a terrible example of Ignatius, the bishop of Antioch, the leading city of Syria, thus frightening the Christians into giving up their faith. He was placed into the arena with wild animals and then finally killed. But Ignatius gloried in the prospect of following his Lord in martyrdom. (The Greek word *martyros* means "witness," not "victim." Those who died as a witness to the faith saw their destiny as glorious testimony rather than empty tragedy.)

During the reign of Marcus Aurelius (161–180), the issue between Rome and the church became much more public and explicit. This emperor was a deeply thoughtful man. His earlier training included Stoic philosophy under Epictetus, who taught that divine providence ruled the universe and that human happiness could be found only by indifference toward strife and misery. Shortly before Marcus's reign, Justin, a Christian leader from Palestine, came to Rome. He had been trained in philosophy and after his conversion had tried to combine biblical and theological insights into the working out of God's purpose (*logos*). In Rome he addressed a defense of Christianity (*Apologia*) to Antoninus Pius, Marcus's predecessor. It was an impressive document and pointed the way for later Christian theologians to draw on Greek philosophy and ethics as a means of providing a rationale for faith and making it more appealing to pagan thinkers. But under Marcus Aurelius, Justin was martyred, apparently on the grounds that his denunciation of sacrifices to the gods was a threat to the welfare of the state. And after him the persecutions of Christians increased, accompanied by subtle effective strategies of brainwashing and subversion.

Various New Testament writings anticipated the conflict that would come to a climax in the late third century between Rome and the church, although it was far longer in coming than the writers seem to have expected. The fact that the Christians worshipped a single God pleased the more sophisticated Romans, who believed that there must be one god above the many gods. And the generosity of Christians in caring for the poor, the ill, the aged was profoundly impressive, even to the bitterest enemies of the new faith. The often-quoted exclamation, "See how they love one another," was not at all a put-down or a satirical remark. But the private nature of their meetings and especially of the Eucharist (celebration of Communion), as well as their disdain for the popular gods, inevitably led the Romans to distrust, harrass, and persecute them.

The Christians' anticipation of persecution, or perhaps their experience of it, is evident in the Letter to the Hebrews. In Hebrews 10:32–33, reference is made to the sufferings of the Christians, the public exposure to abuse and affliction, the imprisonment and plundering of property, although they had not yet experienced martyrdom (Hebrews 12:4). The writer seeks to encourage them to hold firm in their profession of faith by presenting to them the examples of the faithful of the Old Testament who accepted suffering as divine discipline and as a necessary stage toward the achievement of God's purpose for His people (Hebrews 11:32–39). Similarly, the writing known as the First Letter of Peter warns its readers that they face a "fiery ordeal," which will cause them to share in the sufferings of Christ (I Peter 4:12). The end of the present age is "at hand" (I Peter 4:7); still they are called upon to endure until the consummation of God's kingdom occurs. Meanwhile, they are to be scrupulously careful to avoid any kind of immoral behavior (I Peter 4:3), and especially any criminal action that would violate civil laws, such as murder, thievery, or even mischief-making (4:15). The only issue on which they might confront the Roman authorities is their Christian confession, their being "reproached for the name of Christ" (4:14). It is "as a Christian" (4:16) that they are to suffer, which implies that the term *Christian* was widely known and that it was regarded by most Roman subjects as disgraceful and unpatriotic.

The vivid rhetoric of the Revelation of John, the last book in the New Testament, saw the issue of conflict between church and state in far more dramatic form. Drawing on imagery from Jewish apocalyptic writings (writings that prophesied the destiny of the world), Revelation sees the mounting battle between the church and Rome as the earthly counterpart of a heavenly conflict between God and Satan. Employing mysterious numbers and elaborate visions, the author depicts in a series of apocalyptic scenes how God will deliver His people through, and ultimately from, suffering (Revelation 11:15–18). In the final phases of the struggle, the dragon and the beast who does his bidding (13:1–10) exercise total control over the peoples of earth and demand complete subjection to their diabolical will. But through the Lamb of God, the dragon and his agent are defeated, and "Babylon" (Rome) lies in smoking ruins. In scarcely flattering terms, Rome and its leadership are depicted as "the great harlot . . . mother of harlots and earth's abominations" (17:1, 5), and as "drunk with the blood of the saints and the blood of the martyrs of Jesus" (17:6). Probably the cryptic language of Revelation would have conveyed little to a pagan reader, but it testifies to the deep, bitter hatred toward Rome on the part of some eloquent Christians. Clearly the arena in which the next act of the Christian drama was to be played out was not a Galilean synagogue, or the hearing-room of a provincial governor in Jerusalem, but in the capital of the empire itself.

Chapter 4

The Triumph of Christianity: Constantine to St. Augustine

For decades the Roman emperors tried bloodily but vainly to crush the Christian movement. Decius (249–251), Diocletian (284–305), and Galerius (emperor in the eastern empire, 305–311) are all known for their persecution of the Christians. Diocletian finally gave up in despair and retired to Dalmatia (now Yugoslavia). But Galerius, reportedly spurred on by his mother, sought ways to intensify the struggle against the Christians. He was further encouraged in their persecution by professional augurs (those who sought to predict the future by searching for signs among the livers of sacrificed animals) who blamed the Christians for their faulty predictions and by oracles who complained that the ineffectiveness of their message was likewise the result of Christian interference. Nevertheless Galerius finally repented of his harsh treatment of the Christians. As he lay dying, he issued a decree of tolerance for the Christians and urged them to pray for his recovery.

THE CONVERSION OF CONSTANTINE

Emperor Constantine, who reigned from 306 to 337, had two burning ambitions: to unify the entire Roman Empire under his control and to establish Christianity as the dominant religion throughout his realm. During the first and second centuries the empire had grown so large that it was difficult to defend. It stretched out in a large circle around the Mediterranean Sea. Hostile tribes could easily attack it, especially from the north or east. By the year 300 there had been established two emperors. One, ruling from Constantinople, controlled the eastern half; another, centered in Rome, ruled the western half. Constantine, however, was determined to bring the empire back under one ruler as it had formerly been.

Christian writers who became his staunch supporters report that Constantine, as he was preparing for battle some dozen years before he became emperor, had a vision. There in the sky he saw a symbol formed by two Greek letters, *chi* and *rho*. In Greek this may have meant a kind of axe symbolic of Zeus, but the Christians—and presumably Constantine—took it to be the first two letters of the name of Christ in Greek. With the symbols appeared the words "By this [sign] conquer."

The most dramatic and visible sign that Constantine and his supporters had of divine favor for the Christians, however, was not in the clouds but on firm earth near Rome. Constantine was attacking Rome, the strongly held city occupied by Maxentius, an imperial claimant who refused to relinquish control of his western half of the empire to Constantine. When the latter approached the city, Maxentius was so foolhardy as to come out of the city and attempt to cross the Tiber River to meet Constantine. In the ensuing battle, the bridge of boats on which Maxentius and his army were crossing sank and most of the army drowned. Constantine saw in this event the hand of God reenacting a triumph of His people over their enemies, similar to the triumph of the Israelites over the Pharaoh's troops who were drowned in the Red Sea.

Eusebius of Caesarea, historian and propagandist at the court of Constantine, quoted extensively from the Old Testament to the effect that Christians should "sing unto the Lord, for gloriously hath he been glorified; the horse and rider hath he thrown into the sea" (Exodus 15:1; quoted in Eusebius, *Ecclesiastical History* 9.9.8). The victory at the Milvian Bridge came in 312; in 313 Constantine published an edict at Milan which granted religious freedom throughout the empire.

There are various influences which might have contributed to Constantine's conversion. Some historians have noted the possible influence of his half sister, Anastasia. Her name means "resurrection" and suggests that she may have been a Christian. There can be no doubt that Constantine was what we might call a superstitious person. He believed in overt divine signs and the intervention of the gods or God. A cynical person might describe his conversion as a shrewdly calculated strategy to unify the empire. It had become abundantly clear that the simultaneous efforts of Diocletian to effect political reform

*A nineteenth-century illumination
showing Constantine in three panels: his dream
or vision (top), his battle with Maxentius (middle),
and his baptism (bottom).*

and to outlaw Christianity had been a disastrous failure. But Constantine's choice of Christianity as the unifying force of the empire would not have succeeded had it not been for profound social and cultural changes going on in the empire in general and the church in particular during the third century.

CHRISTIAN FAITH AND CLASSICAL LEARNING

In the early days of the empire, leadership had been provided almost exclusively by the aristocrats, and especially the senatorial class, whose wealth and family prestige put them in natural positions of power. By the mid-third century, however, the army of Rome was the dominant force, and those who rose to imperial power were in most instances placed there by the decision of the army, sometimes with the assent of the senate and sometimes in opposition to the senate's choice. The result was competing claimants to the title of emperor, as was the case in the time of Diocletian and of Constantine himself.

The senators and other aristocrats, especially those in smaller cities scattered throughout the empire and along its borders, cherished the ideals of classical learning and culture. They saw themselves ruled by boorish military types and their lands protected by soldiers, many of whom had been recruited from among crude tribes from the border districts like those they were now engaged in defending. The wealthy and the middle-class pagans feared that the culture and intellectual values they admired were being trampled underfoot by the uncouth army. In its origins, Christianity had been primarily a movement of the lower classes, villagers, and simple tradesmen. But it had quickly penetrated the middle and upper classes, as the presence of Christians in second-century imperial and senatorial households attests. The Christians shared with the cultured pagans, therefore, the concern about the preservation of their cultural and social values in an empire dominated by the military.

There is no mistaking the degree to which the Christian intellectuals were consciously indebted to the heritage of Greek learning. This was the case as early as the mid-second century. One Christian who was well acquainted with the writings of the Greek philosophers was Justin, born early in the second century and martyred under Marcus Aurelius, as noted in Chapter 3. Justin wrote his famous *Apologia* (defense) to counter the charges that Christians were (1) atheists, (2) irresponsible citizens, (3) immoral, killing infants (a perverted account of baptism) and eating human flesh (a distorted version of the Eucharist), (4) lower-class people, and (5) believers of irrational teachings. He denied the first three charges but acknowledged that the Christian movement was proletarian. This could scarcely be denied since the Christian handbook, the *Apostolic Constitutions,* deals with the admission to the church of members that included harlots, circus performers, actors, slaves, and the demon-possessed (mentally ill). But to the charge that Christian faith was irrational, Justin responded vigorously, making a strong case for a positive relationship between biblical faith and Greek philosophy. Thus he set the pattern for much of the subsequent intellectual tradition of the church.

Justin had an able predecessor, Philo of Alexandria (30 B.C.–A.D. 45). This Jewish gentleman-scholar had produced many studies of the laws and narratives of the Old Testament in which he sought to show the fundamental agreement between the revelation of God's truth through Moses and the truth evident in the writings of the philosophers. For example, when the Bible reports that God showed Moses the pattern for building the shrine where He was to be worshipped (Exodus 25:9), what Moses saw was the eternal idea of a sanctuary. Beside it all earthly sanctuaries were imperfect and temporal copies. The Greek translation of the Old Testament actually uses the technical term that Plato employed to describe the realm of unchanging forms or ideas of which all earthly phenomena are mere shadow copies. The Letter of the Hebrews in the New Testament makes the same point (Hebrews 8:5) and quotes the same text from Exodus as Philo did in one of his treatises. Justin, therefore, had both Jewish and Christian precedent for intepreting Christian faith along philosophical lines.

Like Philo, Justin believed that God was utterly remote and indescribable but that He had revealed Himself through His *logos,* a Greek word which conveniently means both "word" and "purpose." When God created the world by His Word ("God spoke . . . and it was so"— Genesis 1), He was not merely putting His will into effect, but was also working out His rational plan for the creation.

The same basic strategy was adopted by two outstanding Christian Alexandrians, Clement and Origen. From 183 to 203, Clement was head of the Christian School in Alexandria. Thoroughly grounded in Greek philosophy, rhetoric, and literature, Clement viewed the life of the Christian as moving through stages of instruction. Just as a Greek slave (called a *paidagogos*) guided the instruction of a child until he came to mature insights into the deeper truths of the faith, so, for the thoughtful pagan, philosophy can be a *paidagogos.* In a famous image Clement described truth as a river which is one, even though many streams flow into it. The truth of the ancient philosophers was taken over from Moses, whose writings antedate theirs, Clement asserted.

Jesus is the mind of God, the mirror of God's being, and the model for human existence in accord with divine reason.

Origen, born in Alexandria about 185, was brilliant and impetuous. His father's death in a persecution under Septimius Severus in 203 led him to seek martyrdom as well, but his mother hid his clothes and thus kept him at home and alive. Appointed head of the school to succeed Clement at the age of eighteen, Origen plunged himself into the study of Hebrew so that he might more thoroughly teach the scriptures. Although his principles of biblical interpretation later led him to look for the allegorical meaning of the scriptures, he at one time took with such literalness the saying of Jesus about becoming a eunuch for the sake of the kingdom of God (Matthew 19:12) that he castrated himself. This rash act disqualified him from becoming ordained as a clergyman, although some zealous supporters later ordained him on their own in an unauthorized ceremony. Although he was not so consciously dependent on the Greek philosophers as was Clement, his commentaries on scripture show that something even more significant intellectually had occurred: Origen was absorbing a basically Platonic view of the world and, accordingly, was using the allegorical method to prove that the ultimate meaning of the scriptures was philosophically sound, just as Greek philosophers found philosophical meaning in the ancient Greek myths by treating them as allegories. In his writing about the being of God and the relation of Jesus to the perfect being of the Father, Origen raised complex theological problems with which the church would struggle for centuries. On the one hand, Origen said that Jesus, the *Logos,* was coeternal with God the Father; on the other hand, he asserted that the *Logos* was subordinate to the Father. Origen liked the image of a light and its rays to depict the relationship of the Father and the Son: a light exists only to give forth rays, yet the rays are essentially an emanation of the light itself. The same figure for representing God and the rationality of the universe was used by a group of pagan philosophers called Neoplatonists, whose chief spokesman, Plotinus, studied philosophy with the same teacher who had taught Origen in Alexandria. Some of Origen's Christian contemporaries were disturbed by his teaching because he seemed to concede so much to the philosophers. Others were troubled by his failure to make a sharp enough distinction between the Father and the Son. Still others thought he made the Son inferior to the Father.

THE NEED FOR RELIGIOUS UNITY

As we shall see, the shrewd but intellectually unsubtle Constantine supposed that he could resolve this and other theological issues and thus unite the church. But what is historically important in analyzing the second and third centuries is to observe how close the pagan and Christian intellectuals were on such fundamental questions as the nature of reality, the place of reason in the cosmic order, and the means by which the divine is communicated to humankind. What separated them, of course, was the question of how Jesus fits into the pattern.

Internal Dissension

Not all Christians shared the confidence of Justin, Clement, and Origen in the philosophical method. Tertullian of Carthage, who converted to Christianity in 185 when he was about forty years of age, had philosophical training (especially of the Stoic school), but he thought and wrote more like a lawyer determined to make his case in court than a careful, reasoned philosopher. He insisted, for example, that faith and reason were basically incompatible. As he phrased it: "What has Athens to do with Jerusalem?" He said he believed the faith because it was absurd, not because it was reasonable. Yet he did employ rational arguments on specific subjects, especially the relationships of God the Father, the Son, and the Spirit.

Some earlier thinkers had declared that for the Christians there was one God who functioned in three different ways, or modes. As creator, He was called Father; as redeemer, He was called Son; as a force at work within the church, He was called Spirit. Tertullian insisted that the Modalists, as those who held this view were called, did not allow sufficiently for the threeness of the Christian God. God was one in His essence, but when He dealt with the universe, He consisted of three persons. Just as in modern law a corporation is considered a legal person, so God administers His universe in three persons. Although Tertullian's way of stating it did not by any means solve the issue, it did pose the term *Trinity,* which has dominated the discussion and the church's language ever since. The familiar hymn "Holy, Holy, Holy" repeats the refrain: "God in three persons, blessed Trinity."

Just as Tertullian formulated his statement about the Trinity in opposition to a view that he found unacceptable, so other leading minds of the church recorded their objections to views they did not support. For example, a group of Christians called Ebionites (from the Hebrew word for "poor") took a strong stand on Christian attitudes toward Jewish Law. They insisted that Christians, as the true heirs of the Jewish covenant, were required to observe food and sabbath laws.

An opposite view was represented by Marcion from Pontus in Asia Minor. In the middle of the second century, he came to Rome and wrote a polemic work, *Antitheses,* in which he denounced all things Jewish, including the God of the Old Testament, the Old Testament itself, all the gospels except Luke (slightly expurgated), and all the rest of the New Testament except the ten letters attributed to Paul. The destructive forces of nature—storms and earthquakes, insects and carnivorous animals, the pains of birth, sickness, and death—cannot be attributed to a good god, he said. Therefore, the Old Testament god is to be repudiated by Christians. Marcion attracted a huge following in Rome, but he was shortly put out of the church. Radical as his viewpoint was, it had real merit of facing up to the issue of the origin of evil, a problem that troubled thoughtful pagans in the Roman world, but which was skirted by many Christian theologians. They were mostly content to attribute evil to the demons, but they stopped short of explaining where the demons had come from. Pagans and Christians alike believed that ritual acts could ward off evil powers. For the pagans, these were magical acts employing formulas and amulets; for Christians, they were exorcisms, the sign of the cross, and, in later years, the relics of the martyrs.

Another movement within the Christian church was led by Montanus. During the reign of Marcus Aurelius (about 170), Montanus claimed to have had a revelation about the end of the age. He went into an ecstatic state and insisted that the prophecies he uttered in this condition were the direct words of the Holy Spirit. Among his claims was that the thousand-year reign predicted in the Revelation of John was soon to begin. Not only in Asia Minor, where the movement started, but throughout the empire, there arose a following that included even the fiery Tertullian in his later years.

Still further complicating the relationship of church and empire, while creating serious divisions within the church itself, was the movement led by Donatus in North Africa. He wanted to expel from the church any of its members who yielded to the pressure of the anti-Christian Emperor Diocletian and turned in copies of the scriptures and other church equipment which the emperor requested. Accounts of the confrontation between the local officials and the church leaders indicate that an inventory was demanded, including even items of clothing, apparently for distribution to the poor. The church members who cooperated were allowed to go free; those who refused were placed under arrest. The Donatists insisted that only the latter were true believers. Eventually they formed a separate church organization of their own.

External Competition

The most serious competition with Christianity came from those religions which, like Christianity itself, claimed to be based on special divine revelation to an elect community, though for them knowledge was more a matter of secret information than intellectual wisdom. Of these, two major types, both of which claimed to have the clue for understanding and dealing with the problem of evil, will be briefly examined.

The more varied and persistently difficult was Gnosticism. The oldest allusions to it are in letters linked with the name of Paul but written a generation or two after his time. The discovery in the 1940s of a Gnostic library in Upper Egypt led some scholars to assume that proof was at hand of the pre-Christian origin of Gnosticism, but in fact those writings also seem to be based on some Christian beliefs. For example, in the *Gospel of Thomas* the sayings of Jesus (no narratives are included) are modified to make Jesus a spokesman for the Gnostic point of view.

The Gnostics taught that the spiritual world alone is good and that the material world is wholly evil. In order for human beings to extricate themselves from involvement in the material world, they required special knowledge (in Greek, *gnosis*) which would enable the illuminated to perceive that within them was a spark of divinity. Through the proper procedure, they could free themselves from the evil powers and ingratiate themselves with the kindly powers. Some Gnostics believed that they should live lives of the strictest self-control over all desires; others thought that moral laws were part of the evil plot and, accordingly, they flaunted their freedom.

For some Gnostics, Jesus was the heavenly redeemer figure, while others regarded him as a tool of the evil God who had made the material world. Valentinus, a Roman Gnostic, denied that Jesus had a real body, claiming that he only appeared to possess a physical existence. Those who knew better would dismiss the notion of incarnation, said Valentinus, and see Jesus rather as the bearer of the divine knowledge that would aid the soul to return to its heavenly origin.

The second major source of religious competition was Manichaeism. Its founder, Mani (216–277), combined various elements from eastern and western religious traditions. Manichaeism was a religious system that had devotees from Spain to India. So great was its appeal that even Augustine of North Africa, whose thought and work are considered later in this chapter, was converted to Manichaeism and remained a follower for nine years.

A basic belief of Manichaeism was the existence of two external principles of good and evil. God in the Old Testament was the spirit of evil, who created this world. Jesus was the principle of good, but he was killed by the jealous God. This appealed to many people in the fourth century because it explained the world situation that puzzled them all: how can a good god permit the cruelties of this world? The question is still being asked by many people.

USING CHRISTIANITY FOR POLITICAL ENDS

It was in this state of division that the church found itself when Constantine claimed it as his spiritual home. Divided by theological differences, forced to defend itself against attacks by philosophers, fanatics, ecstatics, and competitors, the church greatly needed consolidation. The emperor was determined to unify his realm both ecclesiastically and politically. In fact, he wanted to use religion as a strong arm of political policy. Could he accomplish both goals simultaneously?

First of all, he restored to the church any property that had been seized by the government. Then he exempted the clergy from political duties. He interfered directly in intraecclesiastical affairs by convening a church council at Arles, France, in 314. The purpose of this council was to settle the issue raised by the Donatists as to whether clergymen who turned over scriptures to the local authorities should continue in holy orders. The question of whether those ordained by disloyal priests were valid clergy was also considered. The council decided to turn the traitors out but to acknowledge the validity of the ordinations they performed. These decisions did not settle the Donatist controversy, but they did mark a new phase in the imperial power to determine church issues judicially. Eleven years later Constantine convened the first general council of the church, the Council of Nicaea, including representatives—the bishops—of nearly all churches throughout the empire.

Nicaea is a city across the Bosphorus from Constantine's capital, which he named for himself, Constantinople. Promoted as the New Rome, Constantinople had a spectacular location between the Black Sea and the Mediterranean, a position of both commercial and military

Modern Istanbul overlooking the Golden Horn,
an inlet of the Bosphorus.

importance. The emperor's reason for convening the council at Nicaea was twofold: he could show off his capital and he could increase his control over the bishops.

In Constantinople the emperor grouped around himself a host of scholars and administrators. Most of them were of socially modest backgrounds, but as one who had come up from the ranks himself, he was able to fashion them into a brilliantly effective bureaucracy that enriched and glamorized his position. At the same time, he performed many favors for the aristocratic landowners in the west, including the restoration of the senate to something like its earlier place of power and prestige. Even his religious advisors were drawn from both halves of his empire: Hosius from Cordoba in Spain, and Eusebius from Caesarea in Palestine. Mindful of the high regard in which many of his subjects still held classical culture, he had brought to his new capital all sorts of classical statues and other art objects. He also stabilized the economy; the stability of the values of the gold coins in use is suggested by their nickname, *solidus*. By 325, Constantine was ready to demonstrate his skill in fashioning intellectual and ecclesiastical stability as well.

Another series of factors preparing the way for the Council of Nicaea arose within the church. In 319, a brash, brilliant clergyman named Arius took issue with the newly elected bishop, Alexander, on the question of whether one should suppose that, since Christ was begotten in time, there was a time when he did not exist. Did he share with God eternal being? Arius insisted that God alone was eternal and that the Son was created by the Father. Rebuffed and excommunicated by a local synod, Arius tried to gain favor with other bishops.

How deeply Constantine was concerned personally over the theological issue raised by Arius is impossible to determine. There is clear evidence, however, that he saw in this controversy a chance to curry favor with the bishops and through them with the church at large by convening a general council of the church. The emperor offered horses and other assistance with travel, and with a show of modesty he served as royal host to the three hundred or so bishops who attended the council. The sessions, which began in May of 325 and lasted until August, were also attended by about three hundred observers from throughout the world. The most perceptive of these was a young secretary to Bishop Alexander of Alexandria, named Athanasius, who later became a spokesman for the position adopted by the council.

The language of the doctrinal positions offered initially to the council was so ambiguous that both sides could accept it by interpreting it in a manner that suited their position. Since a major reason for convening the council had been to rebuke Arius and his trouble-making fellows, a more elaborate form of the creed than had originally been contemplated was worked out at the urging of Hosius of Cordoba and Eusebius of Caesarea. In the creed that evolved, known as the Nicene Creed, the language about the divine being of the Son and the denial of his having been created was made explicit. Those who held the opposing view were regarded as heretics, and a direct denunciation of them was added to the creed. All but three of the bishops—Arius and two friends from North Africa—signed the creed. Constantine took the unprecedented step of adding political banishment of the heretics to their ecclesiastical excommunication. Now the empire was on record as enforcing ecclesiastical decisions.

Many of the delegates returned home profoundly uneasy about the statement that had been adopted, including Eusebius of Caesarea, who wrote a mealymouthed explanation to his fellow churchmen in Caesarea of why he had approved it. The Arians developed considerable support, so that even Arius was for a time back on the scene. But Athanasius, the vigorous young successor to the bishop of Alexandria (328), provided a clear-headed, reasonable explanation for the position adopted at Nicaea. He was concerned to guard against the notion that the instrument of God's redemption of humankind was a created object rather than God himself, a view which Athanasius considered idolatrous. As Athanasius put it, "In his being, the Son is fully God; in his incarnation, he is fully one with humanity." Although Athanasius' interpretive phrasing did not please everyone or resolve the doctrinal issue, it did provide a reasoned, compassionate statement around which the vast majority could rally. After his death (373), however, theologians reverted to the formula of "one substance/three persons," which had helped to precipitate the crisis in the days of Tertullian.

By now the church was firmly entrenched in the empire. An earlier effort by Emperor Julian (361–363) to reinstate paganism as the religion of the empire quickly failed. Enamored as he was of Greek culture, he tried to develop support among the aristocrats and intellectuals as a way of offsetting what he regarded as the regrettable upward social mobility of the lower-class Christians. What he failed to see was that the ideals of Greek culture had so deeply penetrated Christianity that it had become the bearer and transmitter of that heritage.

CHRISTIAN ENDS AND WORLDLY MEANS

The next great Christian emperor after Constantine, Theodosius I (379–395), convened a second ecumenical council in Constantinople in

381. This council reaffirmed the Nicene Creed and added further condemnations of the Arians. Theodosius was not so subtle as Constantine had been about political exploitation of the church council at Nicaea, but he moved aggressively to assert his will. Not only did he choose the leadership in such a way as to guarantee the outcome, but he took a further fateful step by designating a pecking order among the bishops. Rome was awarded the primary position. This was a natural choice because Rome was the capital of the world and as such enjoyed immense prestige. And, more importantly, according to tradition, the first bishop of Rome had been the martyred Peter. The second position of importance was awarded to the patriarch of Constantinople. (The bishops of the four major eastern cities—Constantinople, Antioch, Jerusalem, and Alexandria—acquired over the years the additional title of patriarch.) The action offended the people of Alexandria who considered their city the intellectual center of the world.

Furthermore, Theodosius encouraged violence when he not only sanctioned the destruction of the Serapeum in Alexandria (shrine of the Greco-Egyptian god Serapis and one of the seven wonders of the ancient world) by the Christians there, but massacred many of the citizens of Thessalonica because they objected strongly to his raising taxes in order to meet mounting military costs in defending the border against threatening barbarian invasions. His ruthless actions made a mockery of Christian morality.

DISILLUSION WITH THE CHURCH

There were many Christians in the third and fourth centuries who doubted that the marriage of church and society was a holy alliance. Theoretically, rejection of the material world had been a deep conviction of pagans and Christians alike. While Plotinus, the Neoplatonic philosopher, in theory denied the reality of matter, he did not in fact object to living on a rich man's estate near Rome as the scholarly equivalent of a mistress or a pet dog. But Anthony, a Christian from Plotinus' home village in Egypt, let his otherworldly perspective on Christian faith lead him in a very different direction: in 285, he moved out into the remote Egyptian desert, where he lived to be 105.

Large numbers of Christians were motivated by Jesus' command to leave worldly security for the sake of the kingdom of God. Also supported by the Neoplatonic concept that the spiritual realm alone is real, by the Cynic's scorn of human pomp and pretension, and by the Stoic's admiration of discipline and self-control, they turned their back on society to live the life of contemplation and obedience in seclusion. Some lived a solitary existence in caves or tombs and were called monks (from the Greek *monachos,* meaning "solitary"). Their renunciation of this world stood in judgment over a church which was becoming increasingly affluent. Deeply involved with political factors, the church's life-style was beginning to resemble that of earlier aristocratic pagan Rome.

In Syria, monasticism took an extreme form. Hermits lived out in the open, foraging for food by nibbling grass like sheep. In the fifth century, Simeon, the most renowned of these spiritual showoffs, moved himself to the top of a fifty-foot column, where he resided for nearly forty years, conversing and consulting with those who were willing to climb up the ladder to within speaking distance of him.

The contrast between the increasing affluence among some of the church leaders and the mounting force of asceticism posed severe problems for the church. And these problems were dramatically intensified by the imminent collapse of the Roman Empire.

THE SACK OF ROME

Pressure on the borders of the empire had been a fact of Roman life for centuries. Germanic tribes had from time to time invaded the empire, but they lacked the political and social stability to pose a real threat to imperial authority. By the late fourth century members of the tribe of Goths were recruited into the army and were sufficiently numerous to rally support for having one of Milan's churches turned over to them. Since they were of Arian persuasion, Bishop Ambrose refused to give them possession of the church. In a showdown with the emperor, Ambrose won his case.

But in the early years of the fifth century, the Visigoths (a central European tribe) set their sights on Italy. Alaric, their king, at first offered the Romans a combined diplomatic-military protection arrangement, but the rich balked at the price. So Alaric and his troops invaded Italy, swept down the peninsula, and in 410 conquered, burned, and sacked Rome.

It seemed that the world was coming to an end. Waves of doubt and profound anxiety swept the empire. Was God abandoning an empire that had chosen Him? What then was God's purpose for the church? What had happened to the promise of Jesus about establishing God's rule on earth?

The nearest the church came to providing answers to these questions was in the thought and writing of a brilliant native of the tiny North African town of Thagaste. Born of lower middle-class parents, he was educated in the classical Latin style in Carthage, with the financial assistance of a rich friend. His name was Augustine (354–430).

43

ST. AUGUSTINE AND "THE CITY OF GOD"

After an adolescent affair with a mistress, who bore him a son, Augustine returned to the stricter standards of his childhood upbringing by a Christian mother. Captivated for a time by the speculations of Mani, he became a Manichee and a staunch propagandist for its teachings. But by the time he moved to Milan, where he taught rhetoric, he was disillusioned about it. In Milan, it was the high level of Christian intellectual life and the appeal of Neoplatonism that attracted his mind and energies. Earlier he had been exceedingly uncomfortable with some of the Old Testament stories, but his Milanese intellectual friends' interpretation of these passages he found comforting and useful. The Platonic contrast between the eternal heavenly ideals and their transitory, imperfect earthly copies remained with Augustine throughout his life.

On a return visit to North Africa, Augustine was reluctantly persuaded to accept ordination and a post as auxiliary bishop in Hippo. This town remained the base of his operations for the rest of his life. In 397 he published his *Confessions,* an autobiography which was also a theological interpretation of the progress of the soul in its ascent to God. This work has had a profound effect on literary style and theological thought down to the present.

The work which seemed to describe best the predicament of Christians in the early fifth century, however, was Augustine's *City of God.* In his writing Augustine made the distinction between what he called the terrestrial and the heavenly kingdoms. By this he did not mean heaven and earth, but rather two modes of life, or two ways of understanding human destiny and responsibility. The Christian was inevitably a citizen of these two kingdoms or communities (*civitas,* meaning "community of persons," though usually translated literally, but misleadingly, as "city"). Those who live by the norms of the earthly commonwealth are impure, self-seeking, and bent on shaping the affairs of life to their own benefit and profit. Those who live by the standards of the heavenly commonwealth are concerned for the welfare of their neighbor and for the common good. The earthly way of life leads only to strife; only the heavenly mode can bring peace and tranquillity. For Augustine, the basic contrast is between two kinds of love: love of self and love of God. Human pride and arrogance are at root idolatry: people seek to deify themselves, taking their own foolishly conceived gain as the highest good. Such persons are as vain and stupid as those who, in the words of Paul in Romans 1:23, worship "birds, four-footed beasts, and creeping things."

Although he made an appealing and reasonable case for participation in the heavenly city, Augustine did not believe that citizenship in the celestial commonwealth was simply a matter of human choice. Only those who have been *predestined* by God can take part in the heavenly city. The grace of God is the basis for human beings' sharing in the community of God's people. Those who are God's elect sense that they are strangers below, but citizens above. So far as human merit is concerned, all humanity is corrupt and, left to its own resources, would stand condemned. But God in His grace has chosen some to participate in the life of the heavenly city.

The time will come, Augustine wrote, when God will establish fully his promised kingdom. Then Christ, the Prince of Peace, shall reign over the whole of creation as King of the Ages, world without end. At that time the saints above and the resurrected dead will be united in the fully realized heavenly city. Meanwhile, however, the people of the community of God who also dwell in the terrestrial city can at least commune with angels and saints in the worship of the one God. But those who live now by the heavenly norms will be eager to meet their responsibilities to society.

Augustine insisted that even the pagans must acknowledge that the influence of Christianity had tempered the ferocity of war. He pointed out that even in their recent invasion of Rome, the barbarians had been remarkably humane in their treatment of their defeated foes. Yet wars are never just, he said, and must be regarded rather as an inevitable symptom of human life lived by the standards of the "city" of earth. Just as the soul can find inner harmony only when, through faith, it finds peace with God, so the human family can find concord only when there is peace between those who rule and those who obey, and when the citizens are at peace with each other as persons. The achievement of that longed-for goal, Augustine wrote, will come in God's own time. Then the corrupt "animal body" in which humankind lives will be replaced by a spiritual body. Desire for things will be gone; devotion to the divine will, will prevail. Yet in the interim the Christians live the life of a pilgrim—one who knows that his present dwelling place is not permanent, but looks rather to the transition to his appropriate, eternal abode. Yet the pilgrim lives responsibly, seeking to meet all his obligations to God and his fellow human beings in accord with the will of God. The Christians' life is, therefore, a paradox: they have no enduring attachments to the values, aspirations, and cravings of earthly existence; yet they are fully responsible for the welfare of humankind, individually and collectively.

Augustine's position in *The City of God* was as important for the options it rejected as for those it affirmed. He saw Christian obedience as possible only when Christians were involved in the life of the world, not when they withdrew to caves or pillars or monastic retreats. He gave no support to the enthusiasts who announced that the end of the age was coming next week, or next year; rather, he continued to affirm the early Christian hope of a New Age without setting a timetable which would arouse false expectations. Yet he did not bind Christians to unquestioning obedience to the state, since it was a part of the earthly city and often functioned by its standards. Neither did he offer an uncritical view of the church, since he acknowledged that it often took its norms from the earthly rather than the celestial commonwealth. What Augustine offered was a cosmic perspective on society and the place of the church within it.

Published in 427, *The City of God* offered a safeguard against panic in face of the sack of Rome. At the same time, it urged Christians to act responsibly within society, in terms of both political and humanitarian matters. Yet, in Augustine's view, the deepest meaning of history is not the story of conflicts between human institutions, such as church and state or competing kingdoms, but God's purpose to create a new people obedient to His will. As we shall see, neither imperial nor ecclesiastical authorities learned that lesson.

A mosaic of Jesus, in Hagia Sophia, Istanbul.
The letters ICXC are the abbreviated Greek words
for Jesus Christ.

Chapter 5

The Church Dominates Europe: Gregory the Great to St. Thomas Aquinas

By the fifth century it was quite obvious that the efforts of Constantine and two great succeeding emperors, Valens and Theodosius, to unite the empire politically and religiously had failed. The empire seemed irrevocably split politically. One son of Theodosius ruled from Ravenna (northern Italy) as the emperor of the western part of the Roman Empire. Another son ruled as emperor of the eastern part in Constantinople. The two fought constantly as each tried to increase his territory at the other's expense.

Things were not much better on the doctrinal front. The squabbles continued over the nature of Jesus and his relationship to God. The Council of Nicaea had been a setback for the Arians, but only temporarily. Before long they were a great power again, strengthened largely by the barbarian invaders of the fourth and fifth centuries who were mainly Arians. The western church's response to this division was to make the claim of universal authority by designating itself as "Catholic," from the Greek *kath'holos,* which means "according to the whole [church]."

The earlier efforts of Theodosius to force the east to acknowledge the authority of the bishop of Rome and to impose the Nicene Creed did not relax tensions. Equally ineffective in resolving the conflicts were the councils of Ephesus (431) and Chalcedon (451). In spite of the pronouncements by councils and emperors, the relationship of Jesus to God was a matter of continuing controversy. So was the relationship of the human and divine aspects of Jesus' nature—some said natures! Another attempt at doctrinal conformity was made by Zeno, the emperor of the east (474–491), in his Edict of Union. But it too was useless.

The major dissidents of the time were (1) the Arians, (2) the Nestorians, and (3) the Pelagians. The Nestorians insisted on a complete distinction between the human nature of Jesus and the second divine person who came to dwell in Jesus. The Pelagians, who believed in free will, opposed Augustine's teaching of predestination and its notion of human nature as so weakened by sin and so corrupt as to be unable to obey God apart from divine grace.

The Pelagian issue continued to plague the church for centuries. It was a main reason why the followers of John Calvin broke away from the Catholic church in the Protestant Reformation of the sixteenth century. The free-will issue also created controversy among the American Protestants in the eighteenth and nineteenth centuries.

ROME'S POLITICAL DECLINE

Rome as a city and a region had gone into political decline. The city prospered culturally and in terms of self-esteem. Poets and other literary figures flourished, and visitors to the city were impressed by the splendor of its public buildings and by its public spectacles. The people continued to think of Rome as eternal and had a romantic view of its past and rosy notions of its prospects. The senatorial families were in alliance with the ecclesiastical authorities, so there was a closely knit ruling elite. But they were scornful of the military types who moved into positions of real power. The military alone could guarantee the future of Rome, but aristocratic disdain refused to admit or even perhaps to recognize that harsh fact. Although the sack of Rome had shaken them profoundly, they refused to work out an accommodation either with the military or with the barbarians. And so Rome began a political decline that lasted for centuries.

The barbarians streamed into the empire. The very way that the Latin-speaking people designated them—*barbarians*—derives from the Greek term for those whose speech sounded to the Greeks, and later the Romans, like meaningless stammering: "bar-bar-bar. . . ." The Romans could not accept such people as their cultural equals, and the barbarians' preference for Arian doctrine made them even more suspect. Their impact on the western empire was only partially military. They infiltrated the lands of the western Mediterranean in search of jobs and economic stability, precisely as in the late twentieth century people from the so-called Third World flooded into America and western Europe seeking a higher standard of living.

Militarily, however, the barbarians seized power. The Visigoths dominated Spain; the Vandals crossed the Straits of Gibralter and ruled in North Africa; the Ostrogoths took over much of northeastern Italy, establishing their capital at Ravenna. There Theodoric, with the

St. Peter's, Rome, today. Construction of the original basilica of St. Peter's was begun under Constantine and completed about 360.

support of the eastern emperor, ruled as king from 493 to 526. One of the surviving magnificent churches of Ravenna, St. Apollinare Nuovo, was built as his royal chapel. The barbarians did unite on the side of Rome to stave off the attacks by Atilla the Hun, whose nomadic empire, with its capital in Hungary, stretched from the North Sea to the Black Sea.

The one barbarian group that was Catholic, rather than Arian, was the Franks, who dominated northern France. They adopted a colloquial dialect of Latin as their common language, which developed into what is now known as French. The Roman aristocracy who had developed large estates in the French area continued to live at peace with the Franks, a social and political fact which was to have far-reaching consequences for the Roman Empire.

THE EASTERN EMPIRE AT ITS ZENITH

By contrast, the eastern empire was rising to the peak of power and prestige. The prestige of Rome as a holy city was eclipsed by the growth and mounting splendor of Constantinople and by rising interest in the Holy Land. In the fourth century, Helena, mother of Constantine, had made a pilgrimage to Palestine, where she visited the places connected with the life of Jesus and the apostles. Constantine later built a basilica (a structure in royal style, with a high central section and two side aisles) in Jerusalem at the site where, according to what the guides had told his mother, the crucifixion and the resurrection of Jesus was supposed to have occurred. It was called the Church of the Holy Sepulcher. He built another basilica in Bethlehem, called the Church of the Nativity, at the supposed site of Jesus' birth. Some skeptics think the guides were pleased to provide Empress Helena with whatever holy places her piety required. But there must have been continuing traditions about these sites in a land where the church had an unbroken life from the days of Jesus and Paul.

Interest in the east was further heightened by the mounting influence of eastern-style monks in the west, as well as by the migration to Palestine of one of the west's most distinguished scholars, Jerome, who took up residence in Bethlehem and later in Jerusalem. He is chiefly remembered for his translation of the Bible into Latin. This translation, known as the Vulgate (common edition), included a direct rendering of the Hebrew text, rather than relying on the Greek version of the Old Testament on which the earlier Latin translation had been based. In his later years he lived on the Mount of Olives, as did other scholars of his era (the late fourth century).

Not only was there an interest in the religious treasures of the east but there was also great admiration for the political acumen of the eastern emperor of the time.

ERA OF JUSTINIAN

After nine years as chief administrator of the empire under his uncle, Justin became emperor (527–565) as the able Justinian I. He chose as his wife the beautiful and clever Theodora, whose portrait has survived, along with his, on the mosaics in Ravenna. Theodora, who rose from the lowly position of a stableman's daughter through a career as actress and prostitute to that of empress, exercised considerable influence over her vain, effeminate, but remarkably efficient husband. Justinian's armies brought the lands east of the Adriatic and in North Africa back under imperial control. He even invaded Italy and Sicily, though he came as a liberator rather than as a conqueror. The efficiency of his tax system was hated by the senatorial class in Rome, but the presence of his armies in Italy provided the economic and military stability needed at that time.

Justinian's administrative skills were evident in a wide range of efforts to unify empire and church. He fostered hatred of the pagans and closed down the philosophical schools which had continued to uphold the classical pagan learning. In the field of jurisprudence, Justinian brought to completion a codification of Roman law. Known as the Code of Justinian, issued first in 529 and in a second edition in 534, it embodied his concern to create a Christian commonwealth. It is an adaptation of Roman law, made in light of biblical views on humanity and human responsibility, and served as a foundation for medieval and modern law.

In the field of the arts, Justinian lavished support. Poets, theologians, and historians flourished. But most impressive was his rebuilding of the city of Constantinople, and especially its great church, Hagia Sophia. Vast damage had been done to the city by rioters early in his reign. Justinian seized the opportunity to rebuild with unprecedented splendor. Availing himself of the architectural skills of men trained in the Greek intellectual tradition, he spent enormous sums to build Hagia Sophia in a dazzling new way. The vast central dome rests on the arches formed by half domes, each of which forms the roof over one arm of the building, which is shaped like a Greek cross. Massive pillars on the exterior support the weight of the domes, but from within the whole seems to float free of support. Sixth-century observers could hardly believe that the church was of human origin;

twentieth-century worshippers and tourists continue to be awed by the splendor of this structure. Borrowing the ancient name of the city Byzantium, this architectural style and the other artistic features associated with it are known as Byzantine art.

Justinian's expenditures on public buildings and his military expeditions in the west left him vulnerable on the eastern borders. He built an elaborate and reasonably effective chain of fortifications to the east, but from Syria eastward, Persia was dominant. The Persians, virtually unchallenged, pillaged Antioch in Syria.

Plague and pressure from the barbarian tribes in the Balkans greatly weakened Justinian's imperial control in the closing years of his reign, so that at his death local autonomy would assert itself in the lands formerly under his control. Rome would be free to pursue its own program of evangelism and exploitation of Europe. Eastern Christianity would continue under the leadership of the regional patriarchs, with only a formal sense of obligation to the central authority of the patriarch in Constantinople. And the cultural elite of Constantinople could continue to read, to preserve Greek classics, and to develop Byzantine art in isolation from the military, cultural, and political currents of the rest of Europe. The potential for dominance of the eastern Mediterranean by a Middle Eastern power, very nearly demonstrated by Persia, would be realized almost a century after Justinian came to the throne when Islam began its relentless drive to conquer the world in 629.

RESURGENCE OF CHRISTIANITY IN THE WEST

Rome's renaissance and the resurgence of Christianity in the western empire were due in large measure to a great man—Pope Gregory I (590–604). He was prepared for the role of pope by years of experi-

Hagia Sophia, Istanbul, chief seat of authority in Eastern Christianity. The dome appears to float over the vast enclosed space.

ence as a secular official in his native Rome, as minister at the court in Constantinople, and as secretary to a previous pope. Gregory I gave to his post as pope the shape that it held on down through the Middle Ages. Elected by popular acclamation, Gregory gave freely of his own family's wealth, as well as of the church's treasures found in monasteries, to feed and house those left destitute by the effects of the bubonic plague and the incursions of the barbarians. Both his charities and his administration of churchly affairs were carried out with consummate skill.

Gregory I had been a writer and a scholar. His organization of the Mass set the pattern used to the present day; his Pastoral Rule served as a model for the administration of the church and the formation of its priesthood. With the mounting political involvement of the church in the eighth century, however, the function of the pope became markedly less scholarly and much more secular. Not content merely to consolidate the affairs of the church in the areas already dominated by Christianity, Gregory set out to evangelize Europe, particularly those ferocious, long-haired barbarians in the north.

EVANGELIZING IN THE NORTH

Gregory was probably not the first to attempt to Christianize those tribes living on the northern fringes of the empire. As early as the fourth century, bishops from Britain began turning up at church councils, as at Arles (314). By 400, there were many orthodox Christians in Britain, and the invasion of Germanic tribes into France and Spain threatened to cut British Christians off from contact with the continent. Patrick and Ninian undertook missionary work in Ireland, but they were apparently considered somewhat boorish by the local monks, whose learning was superior to that of the newcomers.

By the sixth century, the Christians in Britain were drifting westward before a Saxon infiltration from the east. When a Saxon king married a Frankish Christian, Pope Gregory seized the initiative and dispatched Augustine of Canterbury (not to be confused with Augustine of Hippo), who began strengthening and extending the influence of the church in Britain. The Celtic Christians, whose conversion went back to earlier work by monks, were at first resentful of the Latin newcomers, but by the seventh century, the Christians of Britain had united in patterns of worship and mode of life.

In the seventh and eighth centuries, missionaries traveled from Britain to the mainland of Europe, beginning along the shores of the North Sea. Boniface was one of these commissioned by the pope in the eighth century to evangelize the German tribes. During this period, the sanctity of local Germanic gods, caves, springs, and tombs was adapted to Christianity. For example, worship of the god of the sun was incorporated into the veneration of the Christian God, whose chief holy day was Sun-day; and the cycle of the Christian year was adjusted to fit the solstices, so that the Coming of Christ was coordinated with the Return of the Sun, on December 25.

Encouraged by the popes, Boniface not only extended Christianity into western Germany, Switzerland, and eastern Austria, but he took a major role in the political and religious overhaul of Frankish territory, culminating in his coronation of Pepin the Short as king of the Franks in 751. Shortly afterward, the Lombards in northern Italy captured Ravenna and threatened Rome. Pope Stephen II appealed to Pepin for aid. Pepin's response was so effective that the Lombards were defeated. Pepin gave to the Roman church the territory he had wrested from the Lombards. As a result, the papacy had secular land under its control, the so-called papal states which survived until the unification of Italy in the later part of the nineteenth century. Pepin and Stephen started the policy of close alliance between the French kings and the papacy that existed—with some interruptions—down to the disappearance of the papal states in 1870.

When the Frankish King Pepin died without legal heir in 714, his illegitimate son, Charles Martel, tried to take control over the territories of what is now central France. But at this time the armies of Islam were invading France from Spain. The Islamic faith had spread rapidly from the Arabian peninsula after the death of Muhammad, the Arab prophet and founder of Islam, in 632. Proclaiming that God (Allah) is the only God and that Muhammad is His Prophet, the armies of Islam conquered an empire that stretched from India across the Middle East and northern Africa to southern France. In fact, it was the Islamic army that Charles Martel met, almost by accident, near the town of Tours in France. Since Muslim forces were extending their authority across the Balkans at the same time, it is conceivable that the pincers movement would have made the Mediterranean lands into a vast Islamic state. But Europe was saved—for the time being. The Muslims were defeated by Martel and they retreated into their stronghold in Spain.

CHARLEMAGNE AND THE PAPACY

The grandson of Charles Martel was to bring the Frankish lands under the complete control of the Roman church. This grandson—also named Charles, or more commonly Charles the Great, or Charlemagne—was the Frankish king from 768 to 814.

Relentless in the pursuit of his goals, Charlemagne was equally aggressive as a warrior, as a promoter of ethical standards for clergy and laity, and as a scholar eager to lay a theological basis (derived from Augustine's *City of God*) for his own role as Christian monarch. He kept in touch with his subjects through an elaborate network of royal messengers and by a series of public pronouncements, called capitularies. In these Charlemagne dealt with themes ranging from how the clergy should preach (in the vernacular and from a low platform, in order to maintain contact with the worshippers), what they should wear, what they should sing (Gregorian chant), how the monasteries should handle their finances, and how the liberal arts should be promoted among clergy and laity. On this last matter, Charlemagne required every parish to set up a school which was to be open to the children of freemen as well as of serfs (persons who had placed themselves in voluntary servitude to a wealthy landowner in exchange for his protection). The results of this effort were mixed, but higher education, which was centered in the monasteries, prospered. Charlemagne's chief educator was Alcuin of York, from Britain, who helped develop Charlemagne's academic programs, in addition to educating the king himself.

Charlemagne's aggressiveness as a Christian and as a monarch was evident in his strategy for evangelizing the Saxons in the lands to the east of his empire. Convinced as he was of the truth of Christianity, he wanted all people to share its benefits. At the same time, he coveted the Saxon lands both for their own sake and as a buffer against invasion by more warlike tribes farther east. The Saxons were commanded to accept baptism under penalty of death. Even to eat meat during the Lenten fast was a capital crime.

The use of secular power to enforce religious requirements was in keeping with the understanding that Charlemagne set forth in a manifesto to Pope Leo III in 796. The pope was to pray for Charlemagne and to support him in his defense of the church against its enemies. Charlemagne in turn would enforce the acceptance of the Catholic faith. In addition, he reminded the pope to abide by canon law of the church and to set an unblemished example of holy living for all the world to see. When Charlemagne was called to Rome in 800 to settle a dispute between Leo and rival claimants to the papal role, Leo seized the opportunity to crown Charlemagne as head of the Holy Roman Empire. This impressive sounding title was an attempt to revive the glories of the old Roman Empire. The idea of one faith and one emperor was wonderfully comforting. The empire included most of continental Europe (Charlemagne's realm) north of the Pyrenees and west of the

Elbe River. But as people pointed out then—and since—the Holy Roman Empire was not altogether Roman nor was it entirely holy. Still it was a useful and powerful concept: all of Europe under one secular ruler (Charlemagne at his capital in Aachen) and one religious leader (Pope Leo in Rome).

On Christmas Day in St. Peter's Church in Rome in the year 800, Pope Leo placed a magnificent crown on Charlemagne's head. The populace acclaimed him as a bringer of peace and protector of the faith throughout most of Europe. Charlemagne later tried to undo the implications of this act—that popes make kings—by having his son receive his crown from his own hands at the cathedral in Aachen. From the emperor's point of view, the damage resulting from Leo's action was incalculable and ineradicable. Henceforth, the pope as successor to Peter had the authority to assign the role of secular power in the Christian commonwealth. The pattern was set for future kings to be crowned by the popes.

In Britain a similar development took place, though on a smaller scale. King Alfred was a kind of Saxon Charlemagne. The Angles and the Saxons had taken control of the land from the Celts and were subject to destructive raids by the Danes. In 871, Alfred became king of the West Saxons and succeeded not only in unifying the land under his leadership, but in ending the Danish attacks. He promoted education and writing with a special interest in the translation and preservation of historical and theological documents in Anglo-Saxon, the language of the people.

Efforts to evangelize the Scandinavian countries met with only partial success. Only in the ninth century did Christianity begin to take hold in these northern lands. In the same century, missionaries from Constantinople successfully carried out evangelistic work in Moravia (modern Czechoslovakia) and Bulgaria. It was not until the tenth century that the effort to Christianize Russia succeeded. In 988, Vladimir and his twelve royal sons were baptized. Christian schools were established, and by the time of Vladimir's death in 1015, Christianity was the dominant religion in the Russian lands.

THE DIVIDED CHURCH: EAST AND WEST

When Nicholas I was consecrated pope at St. Peter's in the presence of the fourth Holy Roman Emperor, Louis II, he immediately began to consolidate the power of the papacy over the lands given it by the Frankish rulers, asserting that "by the power of God we have been born the sons and heirs of the apostles Peter and Paul, and, though in merit far inferior to them, we have been made princes over all the earth." A chance to demonstrate this high claim came when a fierce dispute arose in Constantinople over who should be that city's patriarch and hence the final ecclesiastical authority in the eastern empire. Nicholas's position was strengthened by the discovery during his papal reign of a group of decretals, documents purporting to include declarations of various ecclesiastical and political rulers of the first four centuries. There was even a decree said to be of Constantine in which he gave Rome and its territory to Pope Sylvester (314–335) and his successors. The effect of these decretals was to grant to the Roman pontiff final and universal authority in the church. Although it has been shown that these documents are not authentic, at that time they placed Nicholas in a fine bargaining position for his case as the ultimate authority in the church, including the right to decide who would be the patriarch of Constantinople.

The most dramatic occasion for exercising his authority came during a struggle for power within the eastern establishment which saw the brilliant, versatile Photius vying for the post of patriarch with a stiff-necked ascetic named Ignatius. The immediate issue was whether or not Christians should use icons (painted portraits of the saints) as aids to worship. Ignatius, who favored the use of icons, attracted the support of the dowager queen. Soon he found himself not merely battling the icon issue but also participating in a struggle within the imperial household.

Ignatius was installed as patriarch through the queen's conniving, but in 858 he was deposed and replaced by Photius. Justly famed for his great learning, which enabled him to prepare digests of earlier works that would otherwise have been lost, Photius focused on the old issue of the relation of Christ to God. In his own creative work he asserted flatly that it was heresy to say that the Spirit proceeds from the Father and from the Son. This was exactly opposite to the view stated in the orthodox creeds. Nicholas was invited by Photius and by the emperor of the east to send representatives to Constantinople to settle the disputed election of the patriarchate.

Nicholas agreed under certain circumstances: Constantinople must return certain territories in Greece and southern Italy to Roman control. He also rebuked the emperor for having deposed Ignatius without consulting him as bishop of Rome. The papal emissaries, however, did not insist on the terms, and a council that was convened for the occasion decided not to return the lands to Roman supervision. Nicholas was furious over the fact that his territorial demands were not met. Instead of capitalizing on the fact that the eastern church had agreed to submit the issues to his review, thereby acknowledging the primacy of Rome, he decided to appoint Ignatius as patriarch of Constantinople. He denounced Photius publicly and, in 863, excommunicated him. Photius, enraged, did the same to Nicholas.

In the ensuing struggle, Photius was finally deposed and died in exile, but the breach between east and west could not be healed. The struggle continued for the next two centuries, intensified by the strong egos of leaders in both branches of the church. In 1054 the eastern patriarch, Michael Cerularius, treated the papal messengers insultingly and accused the western church of heretical teaching. The pope's agents excommunicated Michael, who responded by excommunicating the pope. The split was now beyond remedy and remained so for centuries with two churches: the Roman Catholic in the west and the Greek Orthodox in the east.

FORCES OF REFORM

Among the most powerful forces for stability and purity in the churches of the western empire were the monastic groups. Chief among these was the order founded in Italy by Benedict of Nursia in the sixth century. Benedict's followers, known as Benedictines, were regulated in every aspect of their lives: sleeping and waking, fasting and praying, doing manual labor and household tasks. All had to submit to the supreme authority of the abbot.

In the east, the monastic communities on Mount Athos reached their greatest height of influence over learning and piety in the tenth century with the construction in 963 of the Great Lavra. Not only were women forbidden to set foot on the peninsula of Athos, but everything female that could be controlled was forbidden access as well. No reminder of sexual activity was to disrupt the minds of the monks from their holy contemplation. Some of the solitary monks lived in caves accessible only by a basket and windlass mechanism by which they raised themselves to their chosen retreats. There they lived in lonely piety but surrounded by natural beauty. The view from the Holy Mountain across the Aegean to the Greek islands and to the heights of Olympus to the west is among the most enchanting in the world.

Early in the tenth century a Frankish nobleman founded a Benedictine abbey at Cluny. Hildebrand, a monk of that abbey, had served as advisor to six popes, including Leo IX under whom the final east-west split in the church had occurred. The clear choice of the Roman populace, who respected his administrative skill as well as his personal integrity, forced Hildebrand into the office as pope even before he had been ordained, much less consecrated, as bishop. Officially installed as

pope in St. Peter's in 1073, he immediately launched a program for the reform of church and state in the lands dominated by the Roman church. His major targets were (1) the widespread violation by the clergy of their vows of chastity, (2) the common practice of peddling spiritual or other favors in return for a fee, and (3) the practice whereby local secular authorities were permitted to appoint clergymen in their districts who were then under their secular control.

Hildebrand, who took the name of Pope Gregory VII, established synods to take measures to stop these abuses. Laymen were free to disobey clergy who did not live up to these reforms. Many secular princes felt that the reform curtailing clergy appointments posed a threat to their importance. The young German king, Henry IV, urged by his counselors, resisted the papal decree. He continued handing out ecclesiastical plums in return for favors among his people and was summoned by Gregory to appear before him. Henry wrote a nasty letter defying the summons. He was then excommunicated by a synod in Rome, which also decreed that his subjects were no longer obligated to serve him.

Then in an enormously shrewd move, Henry appeared as a penitent, standing barefoot for three days in the snow outside the pope's quarters at Canossa, waiting for Gregory to receive and forgive him. At no point had the power of the papacy seemed more omnipotent. But the pope relented and forgave Henry. As a result, the principle on which Gregory acted—that as God's agent to rule over the church, the pope had final authority over every earthly power and was subject to the judgment of no human being—remained subject to challenge.

THE CRUSADES

Gregory acted in various ways to weaken the hold of Islam in Spain and proposed that a campaign be launched to free the Holy Land from its Islamic rulers. The First Crusade was launched in 1096, with the fervor for the cause inflamed by the eloquence of the pope and the ascetic charm of Peter the Hermit, the potency of whose devotion was matched only by the odor of his unwashed body. With Nicaea (seat of the first ecumenical council, which produced the Nicene Creed) as its fitting goal, more than ten thousand crusaders set out along various

The Stavronikita monastery on Mount Athos.

routes and converged finally at Constantinople. The Muslim Turks controlled the land right up to the eastern shore of the Bosphorus. When the crusaders crossed, they were cut to pieces.

The armies led by the princes (chiefly from Gaul) fared better. They conquered Nicaea and crossed the Turkish plateau, but they wasted energy by battling among themselves over control of the Syrian cities of Edessa and Antioch. Finally, however, troops reached Jerusalem and breached its walls in July of 1099. After slaughtering huge numbers of the inhabitants of the Holy City, Godfrey of Bouillon was designated king of Jerusalem by the patriarch of Jerusalem. The kingdom quickly degenerated into a squalid struggle for power, and the crusade became a contest for control of the eastern lands by the western church, rather than a liberation of the Holy Places.

The Second Crusade was somewhat better organized, both militarily and in advance promotion, for which Bernard of Clairvaux, one of the most influential churchmen of the times, was chiefly responsible. Bernard promised that if the faithful could turn from their petty, regional conflicts and concentrate on the liberation of the Holy Places from the unbelievers, they would receive forgiveness of their sins and God would fulfill His promise of the "year of jubilee"—the kingdom of God on earth. Wearing the sign of the cross, they set out in huge numbers by land and sea. Among them were seventy thousand knights and countless attendants. The announced objective was the liberation of Edessa, at one time a major Christian center. But the attempt failed, not because of the Muslims but in large measure because of military opposition of the eastern church. It believed, and rightly so, that there was more here than just pious devotion, that the Crusades were military invasions by the west rather than liberating forces.

For many people, the military outcome of the Crusades raised a mounting suspicion that the church did not have special access to God that would guarantee the success of its ventures. And the selfish greed and lust for power shown by the knights and kings posed serious questions about the nobility of the undertaking as a whole. Surprisingly, Bernard—whose preaching had been a major factor in launching the Second Crusade—was able to provide a religious justification for the defeat of the enterprise. The failure, he declared, had been God's divine retribution for the Christian soldiers' lack of obedience to His wishes.

Bernard continued to exert enormous influence as a kind of dictator to popes, kings, and ordinary subjects. Largely by his eloquence and prestige, he was able to settle a dispute between two rivals for the papal throne in 1130. But the papacy was plagued by revolutionary movements, such as the proletarian commonwealth set up in Rome by

Arnold of Brescia in 1146, and the resurgence of a sect—the Cathari—who, like the Manichees, believed in a constant cosmic struggle between the powers of good and evil. Their ascetic rules forbade them to eat meat and encouraged euthanasia and suicide. In order to combat such unacceptable teachings, the church in 1184 instituted the Inquisition. Bishops were required to examine persons suspected of heresy (thoughts or beliefs that were not orthodox), and the faithful were required to inform on any whom they thought to be heretical.

In Germany, Frederick Barbarossa, the Holy Roman emperor, was involved in a power struggle with the popes. Henry II of England tried to use his archbishop Thomas à Becket as a tool to enhance his own power. When Thomas rebelled, Henry had him murdered in his own cathedral in Canterbury. This murder became a symbol for the popular revulsion at the corruption of the monarchy. But in 1187 the kings of western Europe forgot their struggles with the church when they heard that Jerusalem had once again fallen into the hands of the Muslims. The aged Frederick and other kings organized formidable forces and returned to the Holy Land. Although they did not achieve total victory, the leader of the Muslims, Saladin, agreed to allow free access to the Holy Places.

Ironically, Muslim power was waning in the west, with the rise of Christian principalities in Spain (1212), but the Fourth Crusade left Islamic authority unchallenged in Palestine. The major results were only to weaken the eastern church further and to place western Christians as rulers of certain eastern territories.

The subsequent crusades included attacks on Muslim strongholds in Tunis and Egypt, but the entire enterprise, begun in 1096, ended in 1291 with Islam still in firm control of Palestine and the Holy Places. The only tangible results were the further weakening of the eastern empire and of the Greek church. Latin rulers took over in Constantinople (1204) and divided up Greek lands among friends and allies, but control was superficial and impermanent. The only thing surprising about the fall of Constantinople to the Turkish Muslims in 1453 is that it was so long delayed.

The most important outcome of the Crusades, however, was not military or religious, but social. The dislocation of large numbers of persons, the breaking up of family and community life, the spirit of adventure that the Crusades bred unrooted the fixed pattern of life in the feudal system. Villagers no longer lived close to the castle walls of a local lord for his protection. Rather, towns sprang up and city governments became powerful as the influence of the local lords faded. The position of the town dwellers and artisans greatly improved. New trade routes were established with the eastern cities, and markets were found for products that many Europeans had hardly heard about but now craved to have.

THE CHURCH AS CHAMPION OF ART AND LEARNING

In the thirteenth century the spiritual welfare of the society was attended to more and more by monastic orders which had begun with Benedict of Nursia centuries before and spread across Europe. Following the example of the disciples, St. Dominic (1170–1221) wandered about without shoes, dependent on the generosity of those among whom he served, teaching and evangelizing. He founded the Dominican order of monks, which had a serious intellectual program of instruction as its base and a skillfully organized network of regional administration as its strategy. These monks lived among those whom they served rather than in a monastery, withdrawn from life. St. Francis (1182–1226) and his followers took a literal interpretation of Jesus' instruction to sell all that one has and give it to the poor (Mark 10:21). They believed that the only way to communicate the meaning of the Christian faith was to live the life of complete poverty, and that instruction, good works, the works of healing would not accomplish this. Freedom to love others fully was possible only for those who were free of all possessions.

A new manner of imparting knowledge—the university—was to become the most significant and enduring contribution of the later Middle Ages. The early university was not like the modern comprehensive academic cafeterias, where there is knowledge or a skill to be dispensed for every taste. Rather, it began as an effort to develop a unified view of the world in accord with Christian faith. Earlier, learning had been kept alive in the west largely through the efforts of monastic groups, but gradually there began to emerge communities of scholars, or masters. Their students shared mutually in the acquisition of knowledge and achievement of new perspectives. At the urging of French bishops, and especially the bishop of Paris, the schools linked with cathedrals grew in size and significance. By the late twelfth century, the cathedral of Notre Dame in Paris was the center for justly renowned studies in philosophy, law, and theology, as well as the arts.

The intellectual goal was the development of a *summa,* a system of thought that would bind in one all aspects of human aspiration and responsibility: theology, ethics, law, the orders of the natural world, art in all forms of expression. There was no distinction between sacred and secular, between science and art. All were regarded as facets of a single Christian universe. Increasingly important was the method of classifying all sorts of objects and ideas. This method, often referred to as the scholastic method, derived from the philosophy of Aristotle, whose works reached the west in Arabic translation used by Islamic scholars of Spain.

The dialectic mode of inquiry and instruction—a method of thought that seeks to move from statement to contradictory counterstatement to a resolution of the contradiction by the emerging of a new truth— was developed by Anselm (1033–1109). It was used by others in subsequent centuries but brought to a new level of refinement by Thomas Aquinas, whose *summa* continues to stand as the supreme model of the scholastic undertaking to achieve a universal perspective on reality. Carefully schooled in Aristotelian philosophy by his teacher, Albertus Magnus (1206–1280), Thomas asserted the fundamental harmony of reason and revelation, of Aristotle and Christian truth. The latter provided the answers; the former offered the way of getting at the answers. Using Aristotle's arguments for the existence of God, Thomas showed how reason alone could prove that God exists, but then went on to show how the biblical revelation demonstrates what God is like. The elaborate method of classification taken over from Aristotle enabled Thomas to arrange the whole scope of human knowledge and experience of his day in a massive comprehensive system. Most of his contemporaries, still influenced by Plato and Augustine, were critical of his approach to theology; only in subsequent centuries did the Thomistic system become normative for Roman Catholic theology. It was in the intellectual and artistic realm, therefore, that the enduring contribution of the Middle Ages was made to the Christian tradition of the West.

Chapter 6

The Struggle for Faith and Freedom

The decades before and after the year 1500 are crucial ones in the history of the Western world. It was a century of great intellectual ferment. This had a profoundly liberating effect on the human spirit, but it also placed great strains on the Catholic faith.

After the fall of Constantinople in 1453, there was a migration of Greek-speaking scholars to Europe from the east. Europe thus rediscovered the rich philosophical tradition of Aristotle, Plato, and the Stoics, although Thomas Aquinas' synthesis of the philosophy of Aristotle and the theology of the church had been exerting its profound influence since the thirteenth century. Mathematics and astronomical calculations were spurred. Reports of dimly known cultures in the Far East flowed to the west. One of the enduring results came through the voyages of exploration of the Atlantic and the Pacific. Columbus reached the New World in 1492. Da Gama sailed to India by sea in 1498. Magellan made it to the Philippines by way of South America in 1521; and although he died there, his men arrived back in Europe after making the first circumnavigation of the world.

The world was open in a way it had never been before. The world of the mind was opened as well. Men like Copernicus were redefining the universe and humankind's place in it. Old dogmas and cherished beliefs came under attack. Floods of new knowledge swept over Europe. The printing press had been invented, and knowledge could be disseminated widely and relatively cheaply.

The Hebrew Bible became available in Europe in 1506; the Greek Bible, in 1516. By 1522 the Germans could read the Bible in their own language and thus were no longer dependent on the Latin Vulgate. The English could also read an English Bible, thanks to the translation by William Tyndale, who was executed for his efforts in 1536. The study of the Bible, whether under church auspices or not, was possible in an unprecedented way. That was to present a profound challenge to the uniformity of church dogma.

THE STATE OF THE CHURCH

The church in the era around 1500 was profoundly split. Not only was there the gulf between the eastern and western churches, but now there was a split within the western church itself. From 1378 to 1449, there were two popes in the west—one in Rome and one in Avignon, France. Each had his own set of papal quarters, cardinals, staffs, tax and financial structures. The very notion of catholicity was made a mockery by the *two* supreme heads in the west *and* a supreme head of the eastern church.

Even worse was the manner in which some of the popes behaved. They sold posts in the church to the highest bidder and exploited human weakness and gullibility to the extreme in order to enrich their already overflowing coffers. For example, they sold indulgences and relics of the saints (blood, hair, bones, tears, chains, and so on)—at least they *said* they belonged to the saints. Those who protested against the greed and the lust for power were themselves harrassed or even martyred.

The papal system came under serious attack beginning in the fourteenth century. One of the earlier protestors was Marsilius of Padua (1275–1342), who sought to locate ultimate ecclesiastical authority in the New Testament and in the decisions reached by "the whole body of citizens" of the church, rather than by the pope. He also tried to make the bishops and clergy subject to the body of Christians.

William of Ockham (1300?–1349), an Englishman, attacked the papal system on strangely ambiguous grounds. On the one hand he asserted that reason cannot establish the truth of doctrines such as the Trinity or the incarnation. But at the same time he affirmed their truth, though he did so only because the church had taught him to do so. It was an easy step for others under his influence to agree with him on the nonrationality of the church's teaching, and then to reject it. Ockham denied that papal power was authorized to interfere in secular matters, and declared that for the pope to make judgments on matters of politics or natural law was to "put his sickle in alien corn." Power is with the people, not the pope, said Ockham; and the pope must be subject to their decisions. This was a stunning and clear defiance of papal authority.

John Wycliffe (1320?–1384), another Englishman, aroused papal wrath by asserting that the Bible, not the pope, was the ultimate authority for Christians. He saw the papacy as an instrument of service, not an agent of absolute control. Wycliffe's enduring contribution was an English translation of the Bible, but his influence spread far beyond his native England.

Jan Hus (1369?-1415), from what is now Czechoslovakia, was one of those who admired Wycliffe's views. In addition to protesting the sale of indulgences, he further said that Christ, not the pope, was head of the church, and that every believer stands as much in the succession of the apostles as does the bishop of Rome. Condemned by the Council of Constance (1415) as a heretic after a travesty of a trial, Hus was burned, together with his writings, and his ashes were thrown into the Rhine. His death inflamed the fires of nationalism in his native land, with the result that the Catholic clergy there began allowing the laity a fuller role in the life of the church.

Erasmus (1466?-1536) was a Dutch humanist who remained within the Roman Catholic church to his death. In a satirical work titled *In Praise of Folly* (1509), Erasmus recorded an imaginary conversation between St. Peter and Pope Julius II in which he listed three types among the "regiment of fools": the priests, who peddle promises of pardon in heaven and who prattle about ghosts and relics of the saints, the theologians, who dazzle one another with "magisterial definitions" and abstruse arguments, and the monks, whose grossness and hypocrisy are everywhere evident even though by definition they are supposed to live alone. All three types, Erasmus claimed, think that salvation can be achieved through "foppish ceremonies" and "legendary traditions."

One could sense that revolution was in the air. England seemed to be full of heretics. The peasants of Germany were on the brink of revolt against the rich and the noble who kept them in social and economic subjection with the sanction of the king and the pope. The Turkish armies of the Ottoman Empire were approaching Vienna, so that an Islamic takeover of Europe was once again a real threat. The fading powers of the Holy Roman Empire, together with the division within the Roman church, led to a resurgence of national consciousness among the people of Europe and with it a desire for local autonomy. The catalytic agent whose conviction, courage, and eloquence helped to precipitate the breakdown of the medieval synthesis of state and church was Martin Luther (1483-1546).

MARTIN LUTHER LEADS THE ATTACK

In 1517 there came to the German city of Wittenberg a Dominican monk, Johann Tetzel, dispatched there on ecclesiastical business. In the church connected to the royal castle of Wittenberg, the German rulers over the years had gathered thousands of relics, including a tear that Jesus was supposed to have shed over Jerusalem. Tetzel came to sell indulgences by which the faithful, on payment of appropriate fees, could assure a shorter stay in purgatory for themselves or their loved ones. Money had to be raised because one of the German princes was trying to bribe the pope to confirm him as archbishop of Mainz.

An Augustinian monk named Martin Luther decided to debate Tetzel on the matter of indulgences, and in accord with the practice of the time, he tacked up on the church door a series of statements as a public challenge. The posting of these Ninety-five Theses was a crucial moment in the history of Christianity. In retrospect it can be regarded as an announcement of the Reformation.

Luther's attack on Tetzel's indulgence peddling was, of course, equally an attack on the papacy which promoted such fund-raising devices. The theses offered by Luther made this clear, pointing out that the practice was contrary to scripture and was incompatible with Christian love: Why did not the pope empty purgatory "for the sake of holy love" rather than dole out pardons "for the sake of sordid money"? An even more fundamental undermining of papal authority is evident in Luther's *Appeal to the German Nobility* (1520), which was shrewdly calculated to appeal to German nationalism and to rally the support of the princes, even while developing his theological criticism of Rome. In this document he denied that the pope should have power over the temporal authorities; rather, he claimed, all Christians were members of one body in Christ (quoting Paul in I Corinthians 12), so that they differ only in function, not in the right to control one another. If the pope or any other Christian abuses his role, he should be removed from it. Further, the pope has no right to set himself as the final interpreter of scripture; the council of Christians must decide what the scriptures intend, including errors committed by the pope. He then went on to list practices and institutions which should be ended, including the practice of kissing the pope's feet, papal control of territories, masses for the dead, submission of civil affairs to papal decision, and exorbitant interest rates.

But Luther had only begun. Also in 1520 he addressed to Pope Leo X a *Treatise on Christian Liberty,* in which he declared that the Holy See (the papal establishment) was "more corrupt than any Sodom or Babylon ever was" and that it was "characterized by a totally depraved, hopeless and notorious wickedness. . . . Even Antichrist, should he come, could think of nothing to add to its wickedness." In what followed in this treatise, Luther tried to assign the guilt for the handling of affairs by the papal establishment to the pope's advisors and underlings, sparing the pope himself from major blame. In the main body of the work, Luther rejected the notion that meritorious works of any kind could gain a person favor with God. One's primary relationship with God, as Paul had asserted in his letters to the Galatians and to the Romans, was based on faith alone. Good works are merely the appropriate means by which humans express gratitude for grace received rather than the means by which grace is obtained: "As our heavenly father has come to our help, we also ought to help our neighbor through our body and its works, and each should become as it were a Christ to the other . . . that we may be truly Christians."

The following year, Luther was summoned by the newly elected Holy Roman emperor, Charles V, to appear at a convocation, or diet, in the city of Worms. On the way there, Luther was greeted by the populace as a hero, but he was warned that he had already been condemned and that the safe conduct promised him by the emperor was a sham. Nevertheless he went to the diet, where he was interrogated by a hostile official named Johann Eck. Luther acknowledged that he had written certain books which were under attack and admitted that he had been severely critical of the papacy, claiming that it had exceeded its authority and taught things that were "contrary to the Gospel and to the Fathers," and that its ignoble schemes were robbing the German nation. He concluded his defense: "Unless I am convicted by scripture or by right reason (for I trust neither in popes nor in councils, since they have often erred and contradicted themselves) . . . I neither can nor will recant anything, since it is neither right nor sage to go against conscience." The emperor sided fully with the church, of course, and the Edict of Worms declared that Luther should be "cut off from the Church of God like a limb, an obstinate schismatic and manifest heretic."

In the long run Luther's criticism of the papacy was not so significant as his appeal to scripture and to conscience as the final authority for the Christian. He mentioned the role of "right reason" and the councils in deciding questions of faith and action, but it was really the more personal factors, such as one's own reading of scripture and the voice of one's conscience, that were paramount for Luther. This was in tune with the spirit of the times, especially with humanistic waves then sweeping over Europe, and it was to have major consequences for the future of Christian theology and of philosophy as well.

Luther also became embroiled in a major social-political conflict that threatened the very fabric of the German nation. In 1525, the peasants of southern Germany issued a set of twelve *Articles* in which they asked for a degree of personal autonomy. Their demands included communal ownership of the forests, hunting and fishing rights on lands not owned by their masters, freedom from the obligation of

serfdom, compensation for work, justice under existing laws, and the right to deal with issues on the basis of scripture. They threatened to use force if not satisfied.

Obviously, the peasants identified with the rebel, Luther, and expected him to join in their battle against insensitive civil authorities just as he had protested against religious injustices. But to their profound disappointment he rebuked them for their appeal to force. Although he found their demands reasonable and even modest, he told them to refrain from violence and reminded them that he had not used force against his oppressors. Furthermore, he was being supported by some of the German princes, and refused to join their attackers. Luther appealed to the scriptures (Romans 13) in which Paul commands obedience to the powers that are in authority as established by God to preserve peace and order. The peasants, however, were inflamed by their harsh circumstances and mistreatment. They plundered the monasteries and announced their intention to "stab, smite, slay" their oppressors. Luther again drew attention to how far his cause had gone without acts of violence, but they felt their condition could be improved only by direct action. They resorted to the sword and were slaughtered by the thousands.

For a time it seemed that the emperor might tolerate the Lutherans, but in 1529 the second convocation at Speyer reaffirmed the pronouncements at Worms. Protests of German princes who sided with Luther were eloquent but in vain. The evangelicals whose movement had spread to Switzerland joined forces. Ulrich Zwingli (1484–1531), the Swiss leader, and Luther disagreed over the question as to how Christ was present in the sacrament of the Eucharist. Nevertheless, in 1530, they presented to the imperial congress in Augsburg a joint and common confession of faith which remains the basic document for the Lutheran faith to the present day. It affirmed the Nicene Creed, the sacraments of baptism and the Eucharist, and the doctrine of justification by faith, as epitomized in Ephesians 2:8: "For by grace are you saved through faith, and that not of yourselves: it is the gift of God."

By 1532, Emperor Charles decided he needed the evangelicals to help him defend Vienna against the Turks, and so he granted them

An etching of Martin Luther by John Cranach.

religious freedom. In spite of the denunciation of the Lutherans in 1545 by the Council of Trent, the German emperor in the Peace of Augsburg in 1555 allowed the German princes to choose between Catholic or evangelical worship for their lands. Luther married a nun, which at first was considered scandalous, but he later came to be regarded by his followers as a model father and a kind of father figure for the churches. He wrote sermons, pastoral letters, hymns, and prayers, which—however incompatible they seem to be with his political scheming and abandonment of the peasants' cause—helped create the atmosphere of devotion and warm piety that has continued to characterize Lutheranism. The range of Luther's personality is evident in the contrasts between two of his most familiar hymns, the militant "A Mighty Fortress Is Our God" and the tender "Away in a Manger."

THE REFORMATION SPREADS

Ulrich Zwingli, the Swiss reformer with whom Luther met in Marburg in 1529 in an unsuccessful attempt to unite the reforming groups, was a shrewd politician. He was able to rally the support of the Zurich town council in his advocacy of basic changes in religious regulations. Among the changes he advocated were permitting clergy to marry, forbidding fasts during Lent, and, above all, regarding the Bible as the sole authority for matters of Christian faith and practice. He taught that the Eucharist was only a memorial of the death of Christ. He questioned infant baptism and began to recommend rebaptism of adults (that is, anabaptism). Some of his associates went beyond him on this issue and insisted that only believers should be baptized. Zwingli did not want to alienate his more moderate supporters by taking such an extreme position, and he ended up agreeing to the persecution of the Anabaptists. The leaders of this movement were put to death by drowning, burning, and being dismembered by red-hot tongs. The zeal of the Anabaptists continued, however. Taking scripture literally, they abandoned their families and, in some cases, went around naked, since the Bible said they were to take no thought about what they wore. Later, under Menno Simons (1492–1559), the Anabaptist movement became more rational, more concerned with individual religious experience, and exercised considerable influence on later Protestantism.

At the University of Paris a gifted student named John Calvin (1509–1564) was diverted from his earlier aim to become a lawyer when a religious experience aroused in him a keen sense of divine holiness and human sinfulness. He allied himself with members of a reforming group that was active in Paris. He antagonized the authorities to such an extent that he had to flee in disguise to escape persecution and possible death. Drawing on both his legal inclinations and his knowledge of Reformed teaching, he prepared an elaborate statement of Christian doctrine by which he hoped to persuade Francis I, the king of France, to call a halt to the punishment and execution of Protestants. Later the work, *The Institutes of the Christian Religion,* was expanded to fifteen hundred pages. In it Calvin denied that Protestant teaching is new, claiming that it is as old as the gospel and as the letters of Paul. Although all human beings possess sufficient knowledge of God as to leave them without excuse for their failure to obey Him, full knowledge of Him comes only through His self-revelation in Jesus Christ. Since God rules over His universe in a fully sovereign way, the response of persons to the gospel is the consequence of God's predetermination. That is why some are chosen (or elected) to faith and life while others are predestined to unbelief, disobedience, and death. Calvin believed that the cause of human failure and death is original sin, which infected the human race fatally in the sin of Adam and, apart from divine grace toward the elect, would condemn all to eternal death. The nonelect, according to Calvin, stand condemned not merely by divine decree, but by reason of the corruption of their lives.

Although Calvin shared with Luther the belief in scripture as the sole authority and in faith as the only ground of human justification before God, his attitudes toward both church and state differed widely from the Lutheran views. He stressed the local congregations of evangelical believers, presided over by local pastors, as the essence of the church, although he affirmed in principle the unity of the church. The churches governed by the papal system he called "synagogues of the devil." With Luther he also affirmed that the civil authorities are established by God and should be obeyed, but in practice he set about establishing his own rigid system of civil government that would enforce compliance to Reformed principles in a stern, ruthless way. Attendance at Sunday preaching was compulsory, and repeated tardiness at the service was subject to fine. Church buildings were to be locked, except during hours of public worship, in order to prevent anyone from using the church "for superstitious reasons," by which was meant, presumably, lighting candles or praying to the saints. Acts of blasphemy were to be punished by the culprit's being placed on bread and water; repetition of the misdeed would result in "some more rigorous corporal punishment." Drunkenness led to fines and imprisonment. Singing "unworthy" songs or "spinning round wildly in a dance" were forbidden, and subject to imprisonment. Michael

Servetus, a Spanish physician and scholar, questioned the orthodox doctrine of the Trinity. He managed to escape from France, where he was imprisoned by the French Inquisition, but he was apprehended in Geneva, the self-styled Christian commonwealth dominated by Calvin, and in 1553 was burned at the stake along with his books. This was too much for some of Calvin's followers who questioned the morality of executing those accused of heresy. But in Calvin's Geneva there was no more freedom of thought or expression than in Rome.

THE COUNTER-REFORMATION

The response of the Roman Catholic church to the movement for reform was generally negative and violent. That had been evident as early as 1498, when Savonarola (1452–1498), the zealous, eloquent Dominican, had tried to rid the church in Florence of the cheap, lewd features that had developed there in connection with the celebration of Lent. The hierarchy reacted by forbidding him to preach. When he refused to be silent, they excommunicated him. When that still had no effect, they hanged and burned him in the great square before the cathedral.

The horrors of the Inquisition were revived by Pope Paul III in 1542. Its council of six inquisitors was to seek out heresy and heretics, as well as those who aided them, imprisoning "the guilty and the suspects." The guilty were executed "in accord with canonical procedures," and their goods were then sold. Civil authorities were forced to aid the inquisitors.

The violence brought on by the Inquisition reached a peak in France. In 1572, Queen Catherine de Medici feared a Protestant noble named Coligny was gaining too much influence over the king, Charles IX. Specifically she feared that he might persuade the king's sister to marry a Protestant sympathizer, Henry of Navarre, which might result one day in France having a Protestant king. The queen therefore seized the initiative to destroy French Protestantism. At a pre-arranged signal during the night of August 23, agents of the crown slipped out into the night wearing white armbands and white crosses on their hats as identification. The palace bell sounded in Paris and at dawn on August 24—the Day of St. Bartholomew—the slaughter of Protestants began throughout the city. Coligny was stabbed, disfigured, and beheaded. His body was dragged through the streets of Paris, and was hanged by the feet and burned. An eyewitness account describes the "wagonloads of corpses, men, women, girls, even infants" that were thrown into the Seine. Old men had their heads beaten against the curbstones; babies were stabbed by soldiers. The bloody attack even spread to the provinces. More than twenty thousand Protestants died in this single mass attack.

Even worse was the ruthless attempt of King Philip II of Spain to force people to conform to Catholicism in his territories known as the Netherlands. So strong was the opposition that finally the northern Protestant states of the territory (Holland) split off from the southern Catholic states (Belgium).

Meeting over a period of years, the Council of Trent (1545–1563) reaffirmed the basic Roman Catholic stand as expressed in the Nicene Creed, but carefully denied the Protestant idea of justification by faith alone. It stressed the meritorious benefits of human works and denied the radical view of original sin set forth by Calvin and others. Although the council expanded its definition of scripture to include writings not found in the Hebrew Old Testament (what Protestants call the Apocrypha), it insisted on the authority of the Latin Vulgate version. Instead of the two sacraments acknowledged by Protestants (baptism and Eucharist), Trent affirmed seven sacraments, including confirmation, penance, extreme unction (anointing for death), anointing for ordination, and marriage. Further, the Eucharist was defined as a propitiatory sacrifice. That is, just as Jesus' sacrifice of himself on the cross was believed to be the means by which God's wrath against sin was appeased, so the priest's offering of the eucharistic sacrifice was a continuing atonement for human sin. As the declaration of the council phrased it: "For the victim is one and the same, the same now offering by the ministry of the priests who then offered himself on the cross. . . ."

Although Protestants had been invited to attend the council, it is obvious that they could have had no part in the decisions, and that the position there defined drew the line as sharply as possible between Catholic and Protestant. Participation in Christian fellowship by Catholics and Protestants could occur only on terms laid down by this council. That basic position was confirmed once again at the Vatican Council in 1870. Not until the middle of the twentieth century did the Roman Catholic church move from this position taken at the Council of Trent.

From within the Catholic church, reactions to the Protestant schism, as it was regarded, were mixed. For example, Cardinal Ximenes (1436–1517), under whom the Spanish Inquisition executed two thousand people and imprisoned more than a hundred thousand, exerted a liberating influence in the church. Yet he promoted biblical studies, published an edition of the Bible in the original languages, and worked for the spiritual and intellectual renewal of the clergy.

It was Ignatius Loyola (1491–1556), a Spanish nobleman, who began to rally a large number of followers to cleanse the church. He began a movement aimed at strict spiritual discipline for Christians. The movement became known as the Society of Jesus; its members, Jesuits. Loyola's convictions and personal experience were set forth in his *Spiritual Exercises,* which were introduced by a hymn of personal devotion to Christ:

> Soul of Christ, sanctify me.
> Body of Christ, save me.
> Blood of Christ, inebriate me.
> Water from the side of Christ, wash me. . . .

A strict procedure for prayer and self-examination was laid down in this document. Included were instructions to try to imagine the fires of hell, to hear the cries of the damned, to smell the smoke and brimstone. Obviously, the intention was to force upon the meditator the grave urgency of communicating the Christian faith. It is not surprising, therefore, that Ignatius' efforts led not only to the establishment of the powerful Society of Jesus, but also to a program of worldwide evangelism, much of it in territories that had only recently been discovered. In South America and in the Missisippi Valley of North America, the Jesuits were in the vanguard of exploration and established many missions there.

A group of clergy in Italy calling themselves the Oratory of Divine Love dedicated themselves to moral improvement and to personal devotion to Christ. Some of its members had a more open view of doctrine and worked to achieve some kind of accommodation with the reformers. Other Catholic groups began to promote works of charity among the sick, children, the impoverished. Documents were issued calling attention to gross immorality and shameful commercialism among the clergy, though the results of such exposures were meager.

St. Francis of Assisi and his followers, called Franciscans, imitated the Jesuits and established churches in Mexico and as far away as central California. Other Catholic enterprises went to India and Japan. At the moment of his death in 1552, Francis Xavier, a Jesuit, was making plans to enter China with the Christian message. Meanwhile, back in Europe, other Catholic orders were seeking to promote mystical devotion and personal piety.

RELIGION IN ENGLAND

England, in the sixteenth century, was involved in a conflict that was more a royal family struggle for power than a specifically religious conflict. Henry VIII (reigned 1509–1547) had married his late brother's widow—Catherine of Aragon, daughter of the king of Spain and a Catholic—in order to strengthen diplomatic ties rather than for religious reasons. The pope had approved the union, even though it was contrary to church law. Later, lacking a male heir, Henry requested the pope's permission to divorce Catherine and marry someone who might present him with a son. When the pope refused, the king suddenly became anti-Catholic. He convened the Church of England clergy and had them renounce papal obligations. Henry then had himself designated as lord of the church. The Archbishop of Canterbury, England's leading prelate, obligingly sanctioned the marriage of Henry to Anne Boleyn. A pliable parliament dutifully approved it. Henry was thus fully in command of church and state in his realm. Yet those in England who spoke out for Reformed teachings and who gave the people the Bible in their own language were denounced as heretics. High ecclesiastical office was available for those who would follow the king's bidding without question. But there was no reform—only a shift of power from pope to king.

Edward VI (reigned 1547–1553), Henry's boy-king successor, was controlled by men with Protestant sympathies. As a result, Calvinists and other reformers came from the continent to spread evangelical teachings throughout Britain. But Edward's successor and sister, Mary, was an ardent Catholic. During her brief reign (1553–1558) she worked fanatically to return Britain to Catholicism. She returned to the pope all the lands expropriated by her father and executed so many Protestants that she earned the title Bloody Mary. When her successor and sister, Elizabeth I, came to the throne, England changed religious directions again.

During her long reign (1558–1603), Elizabeth tried to steer a middle course and thus avoid offense to Catholic and Protestant alike. But as opposition to her arose from Catholic quarters, she moved decisively, driving the Jesuits from her lands and ordering the execution of the imprisoned former queen of Scotland, Catholic Mary Stuart. Elizabeth's financial support of French Protestants and her military support of the Protestant regime in Holland drove Philip of Spain to send the famous Spanish Armada against her. The Armada suffered a humiliating defeat in 1588, leaving the Anglican church—as the independent ecclesiastical structure of England was called—in seemingly absolute power. But in fact there was a large and growing group of people in England who were as critical of Anglicanism as they were of Catholicism. Variously known as Puritans, Nonconformists, and Separatists, these persons wanted a church that would be more demo-

cratic in structure. They wanted decisions to be made by representatives of congregations, rather than by members of the hierarchy, as established by Henry and preferred by Elizabeth.

Elizabeth's successor was James I (reigned 1603–1625), the son of Mary Stuart of Scotland. He had been reared by Calvinists and followers of John Knox, the Scottish reformer. As a result of acts of violence perpetrated by Catholics, such as the plot of Guy Fawkes to blow up the king and parliament, James carefully dissociated himself from any of his mother's Catholic tendencies. He invited the leading Puritans to his royal court for a conference, out of which came the Authorized Version of the Bible, popularly known as the King James Version (1611). It was a monumental translation into the language of the common people and a powerful influence on the development of the English language.

It was during James's reign that some of the Separatists decided to leave England for more hospitable Protestant shores. Among these were William Brewster and William Bradford, who went first to Holland and then, in 1620, sailed for America on the *Mayflower*. During the reign of Charles I (1625–1649), the Anglicans gained even greater power in England. As a result, another group of Puritans headed west for the Plymouth Colony.

England's next sixty years were filled with religious strife. For a time the Puritans were in control under Oliver Cromwell (1599–1658); under Charles II (reigned 1660–1685), the Catholics returned to power and the Puritans were harshly treated. For example, it was against the law under Charles II for more than five nonmembers of a household to meet in any home. This was intended to outlaw gatherings of Noncomformists for worship in private houses. Chaos resulted from the efforts of James II (reigned 1685–1688) to further strengthen the Catholic element in Britain. Under William of Orange (1689–1702) and Mary, daughter of James, an Act of Toleration was passed which granted freedom of worship to all—except Roman Catholics and Unitarians.

Once religious freedom was granted even in this limited way, those who chose to differ with the religious establishment had the courage to do so. The result was the emergence of various religious groups or

Canterbury Cathedral in Kent.
The city of Canterbury has been the ecclesiastical
center of England since 597.

societies such as the Methodists, Baptists, Quakers, and Shakers. In most cases, these began as informal movements within the established church and later became independent church organizations. The first stressed the immediate experience of divine grace in the human heart. Earlier writers such as Augustine had emphasized personal experience, but the Lutherans' concern for such feelings as love, contrition, and devotion helped to raise the consciousness of Christians about this dimension of their heritage. The second influence was the humanistic, emotional quality of faith. This humanistic heritage of the Renaissance is evident in the dramatic, emotion-laden features of art and literature in the Baroque period. The titles of the chorales of J. S. Bach (1685–1750), for example, reflect this influence: "Oh Man, Bewail Thy Grievous Sin," "My Heart, Ever Faithful," "In Deepest Need I Cry to Thee."

PERSONAL RELIGION IN GERMANY

In Germany, home of the Reformation, Philipp Jakob Spener (1635–1705) had developed Luther's teaching in such a way as to urge purity of life on all pastors and to promote private devotion through prayer and Bible study among lay persons in churches. This proposal was strongly opposed by most of the clergy, since it encouraged independence of interpretation by the laity, and therefore undermined the doctrinal authority of official church pronouncements. August Hermann Francke (1663–1727) carried the movement a step further by introducing this dimension of pietism (personal religious devotion) into the training of ministers at the University of Halle. Significantly, this attention to the spiritual condition of clergy and laity led to a surge of concern about the poor. Francke established homes and schools to care for orphans and impoverished children. Gifts toward his work came from all parts of Germany and other European countries.

A similar movement grew out of the migration of German-speaking Protestants who fled to Germany from Moravia (now Czechoslovakia) when repression by the Roman Catholic government there began. A German nobleman, Count Zinzendorf (1700–1760), welcomed them and became their leader. They emphasized inner witness of the Spirit and the purity of life of its members. By strange coincidence—or, as the pietists would have said, by divine providence—this group had a direct, personal impact on a leading British pietist, John Wesley. And this impact was to be felt neither in Germany nor in Britain, but in America, in what is now the state of Georgia.

JOHN WESLEY AND METHODISM

Wesley (1703-1791) grew up in a devout and strict household. He was educated at Christ Church, Oxford, and became a Fellow of Lincoln College, Oxford. He and his friends formed a group dedicated to a disciplined Christian life, which included a set pattern of prayers, Communion, confession to each other, and works of mercy in prisons and hospitals. The intellectual background for the movement came from a writing by William Law of Emmanuel College, Cambridge, *A Serious Call to a Devout and Holy Life* (1728). In it, Law declared that the Christian should do "everything in the Name of God and under such rules as conformable to His glory." Time, talents, money were all to be dedicated to God. Devotion to God is to find expression, not in public worship, which is nowhere commanded "in all the Gospel," but in personal renunciation of the world and its values in exchange for a life of forgiveness, compassion, and love of humankind. Among those in Wesley's group—which became known as "Methodists" because of the methodical way they sought spiritual perfection—was George Whitefield (1714-1770), whose evangelistic preaching had a powerful impact in Britain and America. His rhetorical skills drew praise from Benjamin Franklin who often went to hear him.

Although Whitefield's preaching appealed to Wesley, it was Zinzendorf's Moravians who had the most powerful effect on him. When Wesley came to America to fulfill his task as missionary among the colonists and Indians under the auspices of the Church of England, on board his ship were, he reported, "twenty-six Moravian brethren who endeavoured to show me a more excellent way." Frustrated by his work in Georgia and full of doubts about his own spiritual state, he returned to England. But he never forgot the peace of mind that he observed among the Moravians and the conversations which he had with members of that group.

Wesley's own conversion experience took place during a study group's discussion of Luther's preface to Paul's Letter to the Romans. He later wrote that what impressed him was that the sacrifice of Christ and the love that his act of self-giving embodied were for *him*: "He had taken away my sins, even mine, and saved *me* from the law of sin and death. . . . I felt my heart strangely warmed."

The Methodist societies flourished so that by the time of Wesley's death there were in Britain more than 80,000 members led by 1,300 preachers; in America, there were 200 preachers and 60,000 members. Wesley laid down strict rules for the organization and function of the societies, thus providing structure and due process for the movement.

A portrait of John Wesley by Nathaniel Hone.

BAPTISTS, QUAKERS, AND SHAKERS

Three other nonconformist movements found their way from England to America. Roger Williams (1603?–1683), a Baptist who advocated complete freedom of the individual conscience, founded the colony that is now Rhode Island. Another who shared this view was William Penn (1644–1718), the Quaker founder of Pennsylvania and its chief city of Brotherly Love, Philadelphia.

The Quakers were a quiet and reasonable people, guided by the "inner light" and tolerant of differences. But in the early days of their communities, which they called "societies of Friends," they had experienced extraordinary manifestations of the Spirit, similar to those of the first Christians described in the Book of Acts. Hence the name *Quakers,* those who trembled and shook when under the control of the Spirit.

The third nonconformist group was the Shakers, followers of an English prophetess, Ann Lee (1736–1784). Their meetings were characterized by outpourings of the Spirit in the form of ecstatic trembling, shouting, and singing. Rigidly ascetic, they viewed sex as the root of all sin, and the Shaker communities were required to live in strict celibacy.

THE GREAT AWAKENING IN AMERICA

Even among church groups of the Reformed tradition in America, personal experiences and conscious commitment of faith were considered to be essential. Church membership alone did not guarantee right relationship to God. In the Raritan Valley of central New Jersey, Theodore Frelinghuysen among the Dutch Reformed and Gilbert Tennent among the Presbyterians preached that conviction and conversion were essential to salvation. The result was an outbreak of religious fervor. Similarly, in the Connecticut Valley, at Northampton, Massachusetts, in 1734, the scholarly Jonathan Edwards found that his learned expositions of scripture were evoking unprecedented results from his hearers. In a treatise explaining to his British colleagues what was happening in America he wrote: "From day to day, for many months together, might be seen evident instances of sinners brought out of darkness into marvelous light. . . . The congregation was alive in God's service, every one earnestly intent on the public worship, every hearer eager to drink in the words of the minister. . . . The assembly in general were in tears while the word was preached, some weeping with sorrow and distress, others with joy and love, others with pity and concern for the souls of their neighbors. . . ."

He spoke of the experience as a "great awakening," and historians have continued to refer to this surge of revivalism by that term.

With the opening up of the western frontiers in the early 1800s, a second wave of revivalism spread across America. So strong and distinctive was the evangelical piety that it made an indelible mark on American religious, social, and even political life which has lasted to this day. Some of its influence can be seen in the following: (1) Voluntarism. Every individual has the right to make his own choices and thus shape his own destiny. (2) Local autonomy. In any district or municipality, local authorities have the right to make decisions that set the pattern for the life of the local community. (3) Representative democracy. To the extent that authority must be assigned to a central power, the medium of transmission must be locally chosen representatives, who are ultimately subject to those who chose them for that task. (4) Unlimited human potential. There is a widespread assumption that human determination and ingenuity can solve problems and effect fundamental changes.

Attesting to the potency of these concepts derived from the evangelical tradition is the proliferation of denominations and home-grown religious movements in America. Most of them lay heavy stress on human potential and yet are well aware of the American romantic and sentimental inclinations and of the passionate need for group identity.

Chapter 7

Faith, Facts, and Feelings

In offering his defense before the Diet of Worms, Martin Luther had declared that his faith could be altered only if it were to be convinced "by scripture or by right reason." But Luther could not have anticipated the ways in which, under the impact of the Renaissance and the humanistic philosophical mood of the seventeenth and eighteenth centuries, "reason" would be seen not as the ally of faith but as its foe.

THE RISE OF THE SCIENTIFIC METHOD

As early as the thirteenth century, when important foundations of scientific inquiry were being laid down by men like Roger Bacon (1214?–1294), the announced aim was to increase and improve humanity's knowledge of God, not to refute Christian faith. Bacon was scornful of those who claimed to be searching for truth but were really seeking logical support for preconceived ideas. Custom, accepted authority, and common views carried no weight with Bacon; only experimentation and conclusions drawn therefrom satisfied him. An open mind and the right information are the essentials for arriving at knowledge, said Bacon, and that knowledge was supposed to make humankind better prepared to know and to serve God.

Reason Versus Faith

At the beginning of Chapter 6 it was noted that scientific evidence in the late fifteenth and sixteenth centuries strained religious beliefs. New knowledge continued with the discoveries of Galileo (1564–1642) and Kepler (1571–1630) about the movement of planets and stars, as well as the mathematical calculations of Sir Isaac Newton (1642–1727) regarding gravity.

In the controversy between Protestants and Catholics during the seventeenth century, the Protestants appealed to scripture as their sole authority. The Catholics relied on the infallible teachings and tradition of the church. But now, even scripture was coming under question. There were sharp challenges, on the basis of reason, to the reliability of certain biblical stories. Did the sun really stand still in the time of Joshua (Joshua 10)? Is the earth a level platform with waters gathered above and below (Genesis 1)? Is heaven really up and hell down, as the Apostles' Creed says? The experimental method and the willingness to develop new theories to account for new evidence caused tensions between science on one hand and scripture and church tradition on the other.

The increasingly influential concept of natural law left no place for miracles or for God's direct involvement in human history. The law of cause and effect was seen to operate universally and was assumed sufficient explanation for natural phenomena. God may have established the law of nature, said certain savants, but nature now functions according to those laws with no need of, or evidence for, divine intervention. To the extent that God's existence was affirmed, it was as creator-originator of the universe, not as Father, shepherd, ruling sovereign in a direct or personal manner.

It was John Locke (1632–1704) who addressed these issues in such a clear and forceful way that he set a pattern for subsequent generations of Christians to follow and maintain both their orthodoxy and rationality. His essay *The Reasonableness of Christianity* was a modest, orthodox statement that God had sent His Son to illumine the dark world, and that through him, knowledge had come that God is one (with which even the Muslims and Jews agreed). But further, he disclosed a morality of a quality never attained by the philosophers: the law of nature, which is attested by divine revelation and human reason.

Of greater significance for subsequent Christian thought, however, was Locke's theory of human knowledge, set forth in 1690 in his *Essay Concerning Human Understanding*. Locke declared that human beings are born with minds that are blank pages, devoid of innate ideas. The sensory experiences of the infant begin to make impressions on the mind, and these are then organized into ideas of increasing complexity. Experience, therefore, is the crucial factor in the development of knowledge. An individual's rational powers organize and systematize whatever his sensations convey to him. This theory of knowledge is the foundation of a kind of philosophy known as empiricism. According to this theory, reality is the experience and encounter with the world of the senses. Reality does not exist somewhere in an eternal realm of ideas or concepts (idealism). Although Locke sought to defend orthodox Christianity, one can see how his ideas had the power to undermine traditional faith.

This shift in thinking is evident when one compares the view of John Toland (1670–1722) in *Christianity Not Mysterious* (1696) with that of Matthew Tindal (1657–1733) in *Christianity As Old As Creation* (1730). Toland declared that there was nothing in Christian teaching that was contrary to reason or "above reason," and that while revelation may offer new information, the understanding of this new truth will be compatible with human reason, which is as much a gift of God as is revelation. Tindal later went an important step further in asserting that all that people need to know about God can be inferred from their observation of the natural world and from their own reason. God created the world, it is true, but the perfect order by which it operates now is sufficient ground for one's knowledge of truth—both human and divine.

This portrayal of God as a kind of absentee landlord or the maker of a perfect watch that ran by itself was the main feature of a type of religious thinking known as Deism. In its most radical form, Deism stimulated resentment against the policies of the church and monarchy in France and helped lead to the French Revolution. Although the revolution would probably not have occurred without the gross abuses of the monarchy and the hopeless financial state of the French nation, the uprising against authority was aided immensely by writers who ridiculed traditional religion and called for its replacement by a universal religion. As the great French philosopher Voltaire wrote: "To do good—that is his worship; to submit oneself to God—that is his doctrine. . . ." God scoffs at exclusivism, at metaphysical theories about Him, and at pilgrimages and pious performances, "but He succors the indigent and defends the oppressed." Voltaire, like other Deists, preferred to speak of God as the "Supreme Being." In 1794, the revolutionary government of France passed a decree "establishing the Worship of the Supreme Being." According to this decree, festivals were to be celebrated not only to the Supreme Being but also to nature, the human race, the French people, liberty and equality, to courage, old age, conjugal and fraternal love, to posterity, happiness, and so on. The irony of this forceful move against authority in religion was that the new universal religion was to be enforced by the Committee on Public Safety, whose means of control was the guillotine. All who dared to oppose the committee lost their heads.

Outwardly more mild, but equally as revolutionary, was the American Thomas Jefferson, who favored the Deist view. On religion, he urged: "Fix reason firmly in her seat, and call to her tribunal every fact, every opinion. Question with boldness even the existence of God; because, if there is one, he must more approve of the homage of reason than that of blindfolded fear."

As for the authority of scripture, Jefferson wrote: "Read the Bible . . . as you would read Livy or Tacitus. The facts that are within the ordinary course of nature, you will believe on the authority of the writer . . . but those facts in the Bible that contradict the laws of nature must be examined with more care. . . ." He also said that one should evaluate the Bible's claims about miracles to see if there would be required "a change in the laws of nature." Although Jefferson was not dogmatic, he clearly implied that when it came to a necessary choice, he would side with the laws of nature over the biblical report. His generalized, nonbiblical religious language permeates the founding documents of the United States of America: "The Creator," "Providence," "The Supreme Lawgiver."

Reaction to Deism among churchmen in England was mixed. William Law (whose influence on John Wesley was noted in Chapter 6) insisted that it was idolatrous to make reason the final source of authority, and that reason could not account for the creation of the world or for the reality of human sin. In 1736, Joseph Butler published a curious document, *The Analogy of Religion, Natural and Revealed*, in which he sought to dethrone reason by showing that all human understanding is in the realm of probability, so that the observable process of change in animal life speaks for the probable transformation of human beings into a state of life after death. Similarly, it was thought that since people, by weighing their choices and the consequences of their action, can exercise control over their lives, it is probable that God will reward or punish them for their deeds.

Experience Versus Faith

The most potent and enduring response to the Deists and their critics was from David Hume (1711–1776). Developing the approach of John Locke, Hume declared that experience is the only source of knowledge and that only experience provides the mind with impressions and ideas. It is the mind that makes connections between events and treats them as cause and effect; therefore, the arguments for or against the existence of God on the basis of cause-and-effect are idle. In his discussion of miracles in *An Enquiry Concerning Human Understanding* (1748), he wrote:

> A miracle is a violation of the laws of nature; and as a firm and unalterable experience has established these laws, the proof against a miracle . . . is as entire as any argument from experience can possibly be imagined.

In debunking the Deists, Hume eroded orthodox belief in miracles and in divine intervention in human history—both central features in the biblical basis of Christian faith. He suggested that miracle stories arose for at least three reasons: (1) the stories are passed on by persons of doubtful reputations, (2) they are reported by gullible, excitable types who take pleasure in wonder and surprise, (3) most of them were handed down by "ignorant and barbarous ancestors."

The outcome of this line of thought was to pose a more serious problem for the traditional views of the Bible and its miracles than had the Deists whom Hume was combating. Hume's heritage was one of deep skepticism.

Faith Versus Reason

Immanuel Kant (1724–1804) spent his life as a reclusive professor in the small German university town of Koenigsberg. Toward the end of his career he wrote *Religion within the Limits of Reason Alone*. Kant's earlier writings had sought to show that reason has its limits and that therefore there is a place for faith. Modifying the position of the empiricists, Kant taught that all human experience is received by the mind through certain universal patterns or categories which are a part of every person's mental equipment. What is thought of as knowledge, he said, is actually only the effect of the mind's categorizing and processing of the experiences it receives in the form of sensations from without. But since religion is concerned with more than sensation from within or without and deals with things beyond time and space, what Kant called *pure* reason can say nothing about religion.

Nevertheless, said Kant, what he labeled *practical* reason makes a person conscious of moral issues and actions, of personal freedom, and of the infinite demand of moral responsibility. Thus, he assumed, there is some moral Being who arouses this "categorical imperative" within human minds. That Being, said Kant, is God. Since this demand of moral responsibility cannot be fulfilled in a single life span, Kant assumed that the human soul is immortal. Although this lies beyond the capacity of the human mind to grasp, Kant did offer this advice: "Act only on that maxim whereby thou canst at the same time will that it should become a universal law."

Kant's view of traditional Christianity was skeptical. It is unlikely that he believed the distinctive details of the Bible and the story of Christianity. He saw the essence of religion in matters common to the whole human race. Yet Kant's views were compatible with the importance of voluntary decision and action that had arisen in the Great Awakening and related evangelical movements of Europe and America. It reduced the essence of faith to the moral law within the individual and the vague hope of the immortality of the soul. To the present day, Kant's reduced version of Christianity has influenced much of liberal, intellectualized Christianity.

THE RISE OF ROMANTICISM

Once the central factor in religion was thought to be experience, it was inevitable that for many sensitive persons experience would involve *feelings* rather than *facts* or *reason*. When the great humanistic theories uttered in the name of the French Revolution were betrayed by Napoleon's ruthless suppression of dissent, revulsion and disillusionment set in. Beethoven (1770–1827), the great German composer, had first thought of Napoleon as a champion of human freedom and brotherhood. He had planned to dedicate his Third Symphony to him. But when Napoleon crowned himself emperor, Beethoven was so outraged that he changed the inscription on the symphony to "On the Death of a Hero."

In France, Jean Jacques Rousseau (1712–1778) made a plea in his *Social Contract* for the replacement of Christianity as the official religion by a civil religion. Rousseau claimed that such a religion should be based not on religious dogmas, but on "sentiments of sociality without which it is impossible to be a good citizen. . . ." These would include the existence of a powerful, provident, beneficent "Divinity," the belief in a life to come, and, above all, in a social contract of mutual responsibility. The only negative dogma would be intolerance of a theological sort. Yet, he declared, failure to live up to the social dogmas would be punishable by death.

In England, William Wordsworth (1770–1850) expressed a view of life which placed a higher value on beauty than on truth. Truth, after all, had led to a bloodbath of enormous proportions in Europe. Wordsworth was more concerned with an appreciation of nature than with an analysis of natural law. In one of his sonnets he wrote:

> The world is too much with us; late and soon,
> Getting and spending, we lay waste our powers;
> Little we see in nature that is ours;
> We have given our hearts away, a sordid boon!

His longing for a simpler, earlier world in which direct encounter with natural beauty was dominant, rather than the commercial aggres-

A painting of the head of Christ by Georges Rouault.

siveness and cold, scientific investigation of his own day, is evident in his outcry:

> Great God, I'd rather be a pagan suckled in a creed outworn
> So might I, standing on this pleasant lea,
> Have glimpses that would make me less forlorn;
> Have sight of Proteus rising from the sea;
> Or hear old Triton blow his wreathèd horn.

It was Friedrich Schleiermacher (1768–1834), a German philosopher and theologian, whose thought and writings dominated and epitomized nineteenth-century Christian (especially Protestant) thought. In his powerful essay *On Religion: Speeches to Its Cultured Despisers,* he seized the initiative in challenging those among whom "suavity and sociability, art and science have so fully taken possession of your minds, that no room remains for the eternal and Holy Being that lies beyond the world." He taunted them for their intellectual arrogance: "Having made a universe for yourselves, you are above the need of thinking of the Universe that made you." He depicted the human soul as torn between two opposing aims: "to strive for the establishing of itself as an individual, and to long for surrender of itself into some greater reality." His scorn was heaped on those who "never make a living study of anything, but devote their whole zeal to abstract precepts . . ." that leave human beings with no satisfactory goals in life. Schleiermacher sought to resolve this tension between self-assertion and self-surrender. In his view, true religion was "the immediate consciousness of the universal existence of all things, in and through the Infinite, and of all temporal things in and through the Eternal. Religion is to seek this and find it in all that lives and moves, in all growth and change, in all doing and suffering. It is to have life and to know life in immediate feeling, only as such an existence in the Infinite and the Eternal." The crucial terms here are *surrender, consciousness, feeling.* There is no place for dogma or for autopsylike dissection of lifeless theological theories. There is no problem with revelation and miracle. Miracle is a sign of the Infinite; revelation is a communication of the Universe to human beings and reaches them through their intuitions and feelings. The essence of Christian faith, according to Schleiermacher, is the consciousness of God which Jesus embodied and the feeling of absolute dependence upon God that leads to true faith and true morality.

SCIENTIFIC REVIEW OF CHRISTIAN THOUGHT

Other philosopher-theologians tried to make sense of the world around them and of the Bible's philosophy which equated religion with morality, just as some of the Romantics did. G. W. F. Hegel (1770–1831), for example, rejected Kant's notion that ultimate reality is unknowable and said that all human thought is a process by which Absolute Spirit is disclosing itself. This process, he said, is evident not merely within the human intellect, but also in the course of history. Hegel declared that every idea is opposed by an opposite idea, called its antithesis, from which emerges a creative new blending of the ideas, or a synthesis. The abstract idea of Fatherhood for God, for example, is countered by its opposite, the idea of the Son of God. From this tension, said Hegel, arises a synthesis which is the self-disclosure of the Absolute Spirit.

This pattern of emergent truth, Hegel taught, could be seen in every aspect of human thought and endeavor, including the historical process itself. His pupils traced out the historical patterns by this threefold method, and thereby rewrote the history of Jesus and of early Christianity. Using the same method, F. C. Baur (1792–1860) proposed that the Jewish-oriented interpretation of Jesus expressed by Peter in the New Testament was countered by Paul's view of Jesus as one who freed humankind from the Law, and that from these opposing ideas emerged the universal gospel of subsequent Christianity, the synthesis of the Absolute Spirit.

More influential than the specifics of Baur's historical reconstruction of the process of development of early Christianity was the very fact that he launched the process of analysis along what were considered to be strictly historical lines. Building on Baur's model, but strongly affected by the romantic spirit of the nineteenth century, David Friedrich Strauss (1808–1874) and Joseph Ernest Renan (1823–1892), among others, wrote about the life of Jesus. According to Strauss, Jesus' followers, who were under the powerful influence of Jewish mythological notions of a Messiah-deliverer who would establish a new age on earth, had transformed their historical experience of the man Jesus into the mythical figure depicted in the gospels. Renan's linguistic and historical investigations were remarkably perceptive, so that his story of the life of Jesus accurately reflects customs and speech patterns of first-century Palestine. But the framework in which he portrayed Jesus is characterized by tensions between rationalism and romanticism. Renan cannot admit the reliability of any supernatural events, yet he tries to account for faith in the resurrection of Jesus on the grounds that "he is the common honor of all who share a common humanity," so that love caused the report of his resurrection "to find ready credence everywhere." While he remains skeptical about the resurrection narratives, his discussion culminates in the exclamation, "Divine power of love!"

More skeptical historical critics than Strauss and Renan in the later nineteenth and twentieth centuries would further erode confidence in the Bible as a historical source, but few intellectual developments were to have as profound an impact on Christian faith as the evolutionary theories of Charles Darwin (1809–1882), an English zoological scientist whose investigations were confined to the natural world. For more than half a century his conclusions remained the focus of the conflict between science and religion. Darwin's interpretation of the biological evidence he examined led him to conclude that there was no pattern of purpose in nature, that there was no state of original perfection, and that the evolution of life was the result of chance in which only the fittest survived. No place was left in Darwin's theory for a mind—divine or otherwise—behind the universe, and the traditional biblical view of the creation of the world and the fall of man seemed to have its foundations destroyed. The humanists rejoiced in the liberating outlook; Christians either attempted a kind of synthesis of science and religion or joined forces to combat Darwin's subversive attack on Christianity. Militant resistance to evolutionary theory ended in a trial in a small Tennessee town in 1925. A science teacher was accused of violating the state law against teaching evolution. The trial turned into a debate between the bitter agnostic, Clarence Darrow, and the populist politician and evangelical orator, William Jennings Bryan, who led the attack on the bewildered young teacher. The issue was by no means resolved through the courtroom rhetoric, but no one has had the urge to raise it publicly since then.

The widespread travel of Europeans in the nineteenth century made possible detailed observation of customs and practices of human communities throughout the world. One of the major results of the availability of this mass of new material about the patterns of human life was anthropology, the science of man. Since the patterns showed that there had been similar developments among peoples living in a wide range of times and circumstances, the uniqueness of biblical religion was called into question. James Frazer (1854–1941), the Scottish anthropologist, concluded on the basis of his comparative studies of human cultures past and present that human thought develops in three stages: magic, religion, and science. Both magic and science assume the fixed order of nature, but magic bases its assumption on a mixture of observation and imagination. Religion, by which human beings try to placate transcendent forces, is no more than a transition from the stage of illusion to the stage of true knowledge. Frazer voiced the aspirations—one might call them religious aspirations—of many when he wrote, "It is probably not too much to say that the hope of progress—moral and intellectual as well as material—in the future is bound up with the fortunes of science, and that every obstacle placed in the way of scientific discovery is a wrong to humanity." Frazer's great collection of material on comparative religion is still a mine of information (*The Golden Bough* grew to thirteen volumes in the third edition at the turn of the century), but his boundless confidence in science was shown to be an illusion by the unprecedented destruction and inhumanity of the wars, political purges, and racial conflicts of the twentieth century.

REACTION TO "MODERNISM"

The response of the Roman Catholic and the more conservative Protestant churches to the challenges raised by romanticism and rationalism was varied but potent. Some leaders of the Church of England found refuge from the intellectual struggle in a deeply personal form of piety such as is expressed in the familiar hymn of John Keble (1792–1866):

Sun of my soul, Thou Saviour dear,
It is not night when Thou art here;
O may no earth-born cloud arise
To hide me from my Saviour's eyes!

Others turned to the Roman Catholic church, with its more rigid doctrinal teachings and its principle of apostolic succession as a guarantee that the authority of Jesus was transmitted through the apostles to the successive heads of the church. John Henry Newman (1801–1890), who took this route and became a cardinal of the Roman church, voiced his anxieties in his hymn:

Lead kindly Light, amidst th' encircling gloom.
Lead Thou me on.
The night is dark, and I am far from home;
Lead Thou me on!

The Roman Catholic church itself met the challenge in a forthright fashion: it sought ways to persuade the minds and wills of its constituents to affirm the teachings of the church by adopting articles of faith as official dogma, even though they could not be defended on purely rational grounds. In an encyclical letter issued in 1888, Pope Leo XIII met head-on the growing mood of liberation from tradition in religion by declaring that liberty is possible only where there is knowledge, and that knowledge must be structured by laws, the highest of which is preserved by and interpreted through the church. True liberty does not consist "in every man doing what he pleases, for this would simply end in turmoil and confusion" but in obedience to "the eternal law of God" which is "the sole standard and rule of human liberty. . . ." In 1854, under Pope Pius IX, Catholics were required to affirm the doctrine that Mary, "from the first instant of her conception" had been "preserved free from all stain of original sin. . . ." That is, none of the corrupting influence of sexual relations, as viewed by the Catholic church, was to be assigned to Mary in the act by which Jesus was conceived in her womb. Pius IX followed this in 1864 by a Syllabus of Errors, in which the errors of modernism were defined, ranging from freedom of choice in religious matters to socialism, communism, divorce, the limitation of the church's power to religious questions, and tolerance of non-Catholic public worship in predominantly Catholic countries. The First Vatican Council in 1870 declared as binding on all Catholics the doctrine of the infallibility of the pope. And as late as 1950, Pope Pius XII set forth as official dogma that Mary, at death, was taken up bodily into heaven, thus freeing her of the necessity of waiting with the other faithful for the resurrection of the dead at the last day. These pronouncements and dogmas served to require Catholics to acknowledge what the Syllabus of Errors explicitly condemned: that human reason was in error to regard itself "as the master rule by which man can and ought to arrive at the knowledge of all truths of every kind."

The Protestants reacted to rationalism, romanticism, and relativism in two quite different ways. Liberal Protestants took the reductionist route, by which the Christian faith was stripped down to its essence. That point of view found classic expression in a famous, oft-printed address by Henry Drummond (1851–1897), "The Greatest Thing in the World," delivered in 1889. The theme was love, which he saw as the central reality of the New Testament and of Christian faith and life. Although he began his public career with the aim of reconciling science and religion, Drummond later allied himself with the revivalist movement—the other route.

Revivalism had a resurgence in America in the early nineteenth century and reached its peak in the United States and Great Britain under the American evangelist, Dwight L. Moody (1837–1899). For Moody—as for his predecessors Charles G. Finney (1792–1875), evangelist and later president of Oberlin College, and Peter Cartwright (1785–1872), who evangelized the western frontiers—Christian faith was essentially the penitential faith of the individual. One must acknowledge his sin and his need of divine forgiveness; in accepting Christ as Savior, a new life in grace is received, which may be called "salvation" or "the new birth."

Evangelicalism, especially in America, soon developed its own institutions, in the form of Bible schools and Bible conferences. Regarding the main-line Protestant churches, and especially the Roman Catholic church, as having departed from the true faith and as instruments of diabolical error, evangelicals formed their own individual churches and, in some cases, even their own denominations. Liberal Protestants, on the other hand, became increasingly concerned about the interrelationship between the kingdom of God, whose coming Jesus had proclaimed, and the injustice that characterized society. Sensitivity toward social evil, especially urban problems, and the effort to deal with them by appeal to the gospel tradition are set forth in a hymn by Frank Mason North (1850–1935):

> Where cross the crowded ways of life,
> Where sound the cries of race and clan,
> Above the noise of selfish strife
> We hear thy voice, O Son of Man.

> In haunts of wretchedness and need,
> On shadowed thresholds dark with fears,
> From paths where hide the lures of greed
> We catch the vision of Thy tears.

In the twentieth century, the term *social gospel* became a central force in liberal Protestantism, with the leaders of the movement taking active roles in civic reform, in social legislation, and, in more recent times, in behalf of racial equality and movements in support of peace. The work of Martin Luther King, Jr., in the civil rights movement represents the transformation of the individual into the social gospel, not only in King's own black Protestant experience and in his theological training at a liberal Protestant theological school (Boston University), but in the support that he developed from liberal clergy and laity throughout the country. It is not surprising that, as white urban and campus liberals joined the oppressed southern blacks in the March on Montgomery to demand equal rights for blacks everywhere, the song they sang was the black spiritual "We Shall Overcome."

THE MISSIONARY THRUST AND THE ECUMENICAL MOVEMENT

Concurrent with the revivalist movements in Britain and America in the nineteenth century was the surge of missionary activity throughout the world, spurred by the evangelicals at first but stimulated by the liberal Protestants as well later on. Although Roman Catholics had carried on missionary activity in the Far East since the mid-sixteenth century through the Jesuits, it was only in the late eighteenth century that a self-taught cobbler, William Carey (1761–1834), initiated what was to become the modern Protestant missionary movement. This movement flourished in the nineteenth century and gave rise to the ecumenical movement of the twentieth century.

Carey was profoundly influenced by Jonathan Edward's account of the brief career of David Brainerd (1718–1747), who sought to evangelize the Indians of New England. Having taught himself the biblical languages as well as several modern languages, Carey organized financial support and set out with his wife and large family for India. There he learned Bengali well enough to translate first the New Testament and then the entire Bible into that major language of India. Influenced by his heroic efforts and by reports of the results of his work, missionary societies were formed and sent missionaries to the Far East and to the islands of the South Pacific.

In 1808, at a prayer meeting held reportedly under a haystack during a storm, a group of students at Williams College banded together to launch the American counterpart of the British missionary endeavor. Societies for world evangelism were soon drawn up across denominational lines. Most notable among these early American missionaries was Adoniram Judson (1788–1850), who worked effectively in Burma and produced Christian literature and, in 1834, a Burmese Bible. After similar enterprises were launched by Christians in other countries, especially in Western Europe, cooperation among the churches and among students aiming toward careers in the mission field led, in the later decades of the nineteenth century, to the formation of the international Student Volunteer Movement and, in 1891, to the World Student Christian Federation. By 1921 the International Missionary Council had been formed to coordinate evangelistic activities worldwide. Through these associations there arose growing interest in bringing the Christian churches throughout the world into some sort of voluntary, cooperative association. As early as 1908, the major Protestant bodies joined together in the Federal Council of Churches; in 1950, the association of denominations, together with various interdenominational agencies, combined to form the National Council of Churches in the U.S.A., with its offices of cooperation and communication in the Interchurch Center in New York City. In 1948, an analogous association of Protestant and Orthodox churches—the World Council of Churches—was created at Amster-

Christian missionaries are active worldwide.
This missionary's work has taken him to Zaire, Africa.

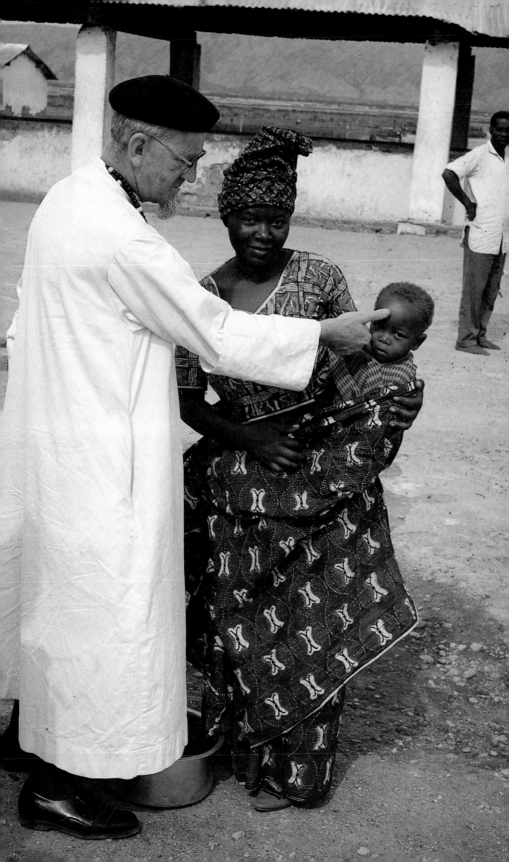

dam. This movement toward interchurch cooperation called itself by one of the Greek words for world, *oikoumene;* hence it has been known as the ecumenical movement.

The most dramatic ecumenical move, however, was from an unexpected source. In 1960, the venerable, amiable Pope John XXIII took the unprecedented action of creating a new unit within the papal administrative structure: the Secretariat for Promoting Christian Unity. Observers began to attend the ecumenical gatherings which were largely Protestant. Leading figures among Protestants were granted audiences with the pope. Pope John convened the Second Vatican Council in 1962, and it was immediately apparent that the winds of change were blowing through the Roman Catholic church. Cooperative efforts were encouraged in theological and biblical studies. Translations of the Bible into the modern languages of the people were fostered by the church. Church worship and study activities were carried out jointly with Protestants. Mass and the liturgy were celebrated in the common language, rather than in Latin. The twang of guitars was heard in chancels as folk masses were celebrated. Nuns and priests abandoned clerical garb and became visually indistinguishable from lay persons. Marriage among Catholic clergy became rather common, with some abandoning the church entirely and others assuming semiofficial roles as teachers in church-related institutions. The word that Pope John XXIII had used to characterize what he wanted to happen to the church was wholly appropriate: *aggiornamento,* bringing the life of the church "up to the present day."

Inevitably the moves toward ecumenicity and *aggiornamento* met resistance from both Catholic and non-Catholic quarters. Conservative elements in the Protestant churches and in the nondenominational groups denounced both the Protestants joining together in church councils and agencies and the rapprochement between Protestants and Catholics as yet another stage in the Devil's takeover of Christendom. Conservatives began to form organizations parallel to the ecumenical agencies—the National Association of Evangelicals and the International Council of Christian Churches—presumably with the implication that churches affiliated with the World Council were not Christian. Conservative Catholics worked for a return to the familiar, traditional Latin of the mass and the older forms of the liturgy. But with the publication of officially sanctioned modern speech translations of the Bible—especially the Jerusalem Bible—and of commentaries and study aids for Catholic lay persons, the movement toward freer inquiry and private interpretation of the Bible and theology was irreversible.

CATHOLIC-PROTESTANT RECONCILIATION

In America it was, ironically, the election of a Roman Catholic president, John F. Kennedy (1917–1963), which seemed to lay to rest the issue of the Roman Catholic church's potential dominance of the state. In the late nineteenth and early twentieth centuries, the power of ethnic groups of Roman Catholic orientation over big city governments led many Protestants to assume that "the pope will rule America if we have a Catholic in the White House." It was this line of argument that helped defeat Alfred E. Smith in 1928, and which narrowed the slim margin by which Kennedy was elected in 1960. But the issue proved to be phony; the Kennedy administration's program was dominated by humanitarian concerns, not by ecclesiastical influence. Even the potentially explosive matter of indirect support of parochial schools by public funds, as in public funding for transportation of pupils to church-related schools, proved to be noncontroversial. In the traditional language, the wall of separation between church and state was not breached.

In the late twentieth century Protestant and Catholic churches were able to join together in worship and study, in humanitarian enterprises, and in forms of protest against social injustice. Where they were not able to find common ground was in the realm of doctrine. Part of the price of inclusiveness was the broadening of the definition of faith. A variety of creeds, including some of the do-it-yourself variety, was in use among the churches, both Catholic and Protestant. Back in New Testament times the writer of the Letter to the Ephesians coined the neat phrase to epitomize the unity of the church: "One Lord, one faith, one baptism" (Ephesians 4:5). Nearly two millennia after its beginning, the church was not agreed about baptism, whether it should be administered to children (on the analogy of circumcision, as is the Jewish sign of the covenant) or to believers, as an outward sign of faith. Nor was it agreed about faith, especially on the question of what are the detailed essentials of Christian doctrine. What it did regard itself as sharing, however, was its acknowledgment that Jesus, its founding figure, was "Lord." The Letter to the Ephesians continues, "One God and Father of us all." The unity of the church was seen in ecumenical circles to be grounded, therefore, on the common confession of Jesus as the agent of God's self-disclosure to humankind and as the instrument of God's exercise of His sovereignty over His people, and through them, over His creation. What is probably the earliest Christian confession—quoted by Paul in Philippians 2:11—has become also the most contemporary: "Jesus Christ is Lord."

Chapter 8

Prospects for Christianity in the Late Twentieth Century

The despairing pronouncement of Emperor Julian which opened this book has proved to be only half true. The Galilean did win over the Roman Empire. The Christian church did triumph there. It even spread throughout the world. But it did not sweep the field. The diversity of Christianity was at once a strength, leading to inclusiveness, and a weakness, diminishing its focus and force.

As the last quarter of the twentieth century began, Christianity was, as it had been from its inception, in a state of change and adaptation. Almost none of the old distinctions held true. Catholics and Protestants were cooperating and sharing in a manner unheard of since the Reformation. But the continuing conflict between Catholics and Protestants in Northern Ireland is a reminder of past hostilities and of the fierce political form that religious disagreements can still assume.

EMERGING FEATURES OF CHRISTIANITY

With increased depersonalization of society—reflected in the fact that people are now primarily identified by a Social Security number, that more and more private information about people can be stored in a computer storage bank—churches have begun to turn their attention to matters of interpersonal relationships. This may be one of the reasons that the decline in membership and active participation in church life which accelerated during the sixties has begun to level off. Those who remained in the churches have become more active and

International charismatic conference of 1975, Rome.

more deeply committed. Many meet in small groups to study and to share mutual concerns. Thus the ancient Christian notion of *koinōnia* (sharing, participation, community, fellowship) has become again a significant feature of Christianity.

Another emerging feature of Christianity is the freedom given in the churches to express personal, especially emotional, feelings. The primitive Christian experience of charismatic gifts (ecstatic experiences, attributed to the Spirit of God, and manifesting themselves in extraordinary speech, bodily motions, or alleged powers of healing) is becoming common in both Protestant and Catholic churches, even among sophisticated and urbane members. Charismatic conferences have attracted tens of thousands, who believe they are actually sharing in the work of God's Spirit in the world.

GROWTH OF SECTS

The hippy movement of the sixties was itself a manifestation of the widespread yearning for personal encounter and identity. Perhaps it was also a reflection of the breakdown of the family which had for so many centuries provided social and psychological security. As an extension of that movement, with its communal way of life, there was a surge of sects. Some of these were based on vague notions of nature worship. Others were derived from Eastern religions, especially Buddhism. The Hare Krishna movement, with its distinctive pinkish robes and shaved heads, offered a firm sense of group identity and escape from an otherwise meaningless existence for a bored, disillusioned generation. The followers of Sun Myung Moon were apparently attracted by the strict discipline of the group which provided them a sense of purpose and security in an era when many families were devoid of love or loyalty or disciplined obligation.

In the Christian tradition of the seventies, however, it is the Jesus people who seem to believe that they have recovered the purpose and group identity that characterized the first Christians. The appeal of the Jesus movement knows neither social, economic, nor cultural limits. Among its adherents are the simple and the sophisticated, the alienated and the high achievers, the drifters and the affluent. The fundamental values of love and acceptance, of acknowledgment of guilt and reconciliation, that dominate the New Testament have been discovered afresh by the new wave of converts to evangelical Christianity. The latest methods of mass communication and the suavest kinds of popular appeal are employed, in the confidence that seemingly secular means can be sanctified when used in the cause of the Christian faith.

The contemporary preference for affirmation over analysis and for radical separation of the business of the marketplace from the business of the soul is evident in the steady growth of the evangelical churches, and especially of their educational institutions. While older theological institutions are shrinking or merging, the Bible schools and colleges are setting records for enrollment and are building glittering new campuses, as at Oral Roberts University in Oklahoma. Evangelistic enterprises have become multimillion-dollar businesses, with loyal supporters willing to provide nearly unlimited funds.

INFLUENCE OF COMMUNISM

One of the chief antagonists of Christianity has been Communism, especially outside of the United States. Originating as a secular version of Hegel's progress of the Absolute Spirit throughout history (dialectical philosophy), the communistic dogma of Karl Marx (1818–1883) and Friedrich Engels (1820–1895) pictured the history of the human race as a continual conflict between the classes—the exploiters and the exploited. All religion, declared Marx, was the "opiate" of the masses. By this he meant that the ruling classes used the power of religion to keep the masses poor and frightened.

Still the Communists treat their beliefs exactly as if Communism were a religion. In fact, it is. According to Communist doctrine, the struggle between the oppressor and oppressed will result in the secular equivalent of the kingdom of God: a classless society in which all conflict would be resolved and in which the poor would inherit the earth. The Communist movement has its own equivalent of the ecclesiastical hierarchy which makes pronouncements binding on the adherents (or those subject to them). It has its own holy places (for example, Lenin's tomb) and its saints (Lenin, Mao, Marx). It has its great festivals (May Day, the October Revolution), its mass revival meetings in Red Square, and its sacred scriptures (the writings of Marx and the thoughts of Chairman Mao). The movement has even undergone the equivalent of the Reformation. National Communist parties have emerged and are determined to assert and maintain independence from the pronouncements of the self-styled central authority at Moscow. This recalls the actions of England and Germany against the power of the pope at Rome during the Reformation.

In keeping with the refusal of Christianity in the later twentieth century to remain in the neater categories of an earlier period, many thoughtful Christians are impressed by basic aspects of the Communist (Marxist) analysis of social ills, and are seeking a synthesis of Christianity and Marxism. They admit the power of economic factors in shaping human life, and they see the effects of socioeconomic forces on the development of Christianity itself. But although they agree with some of Marx's diagnosis of the human situation, they seek solutions to these universal human problems through the Christian tradition.

JEWISH-CHRISTIAN RELATIONS

As an outgrowth of the horrors of the Nazi period in Germany, when many Christians stood silently by or even participated in Hitler's slaughter of the Jews, Christians have sought to foster understanding of Judaism and to open new lines of communication with Jews. Studies of anti-Semitism and the Jewish Holocaust in the mid-twentieth century have begun to appear in religious studies programs at universities and theological schools. Even some conservative Christians have become strong supporters of the Zionist movement and the State of Israel. They believe that this development is an important stage in the preparations for the millennial End of the Age foretold by biblical prophets.

As a result of this interest in Judaism, Christians have become more sensitive to the anti-Semitic tendencies that have been embedded in the Christian tradition from its beginnings. These tendencies are evident in the outcry attributed to the Jewish populace at the trial of Jesus: "His blood be on us and on our children" (Matthew 27:25). Critical historians recognize in this declaration an echo of the fierce conflict between Jews and Christians in the first century, rather than a verbatim report of the trial itself.

Candor and compassion in examining this historical aspect of Jewish-Christian relations may increase the sense of common heritage and human frailty from which both religions developed from the first century to the present. Both took shape in opposition to the other; without the other, neither Judaism nor Christianity would have taken the historical form that they did in fact take. Yet both share a rich common heritage in the law and in the prophets of ancient Israel. Recent discoveries, such as the Dead Sea Scrolls, and recent examination of neglected Jewish documents have shown how diverse Judaism was in the time of Jesus. Thus there is much rich source material to suggest historical explanations as to how and why primitive Christianity emerged on Jewish soil and then went on to exert religious, political, and cultural influence throughout a world far more complex and vast than the apostles or even Julian ever dreamed.

Glossary

amulet. An object, such as a necklace or bracelet, worn as a charm against evil.

Antioch. The capital city of the Seleucid kings (who ruled over Syria and Palestine from 312 B.C. to 42 B.C.), located near the Orontes River in northwest Syria. By the year A.D. 40, it was a center for the spread of Christianity.

apocalpytic, apocalypse. A form of prophetic writing which, by means of visions and mysterious revelations, foretells the future of God's purpose; it regularly includes accounts of the defeat of the powers of evil and vindication of the righteous people of God. The Book of Daniel in the Old Testament and the Book of Revelation in the New Testament are outstanding examples of this type of writing.

apology. From a Greek word meaning "defense," in the sense of a reasoned defense of a religious or philosophical teaching or proposition. Paul's address on the Areopagus in Athens (Acts 17) is an example of an apology.

apostle. From a Greek word meaning "sent." The word was used in the early church to designate those leaders who were believed to have been specially commissioned and empowered by the risen Christ to carry on his work. The list of apostles is not identical with that of Jesus' twelve disciples, since Paul was included among the apostles and because of Judas' defection, but there is a strong tradition that there were twelve apostles.

Apostles' Creed. The name usually given to a creed that developed very early in the church and was expanded in the fourth and fifth centuries in connection with the disputes over the relationship of Father, Son, and Spirit. It continues in wide use among both Catholics and Protestants.

baptism. The rite of ceremonial washing, probably by immersion, which may have originated as an act of purification in anticipation of the divine judgment for sin that was thought to be imminent, but it became among the early Christians a rite of initiation, serving a function similar to that of circumcision among Jews.

bishop. The English word is a corruption of the Greek word *episkopos,* meaning "overseer." It was used at first to designate men in positions of leadership in local churches, but came to be reserved for the single person at the head of a church in a particular city or locality.

canon law. As the church became increasingly organized, it developed its own system of rules and regulations concerning marriage, property, worship, membership, and so on. The Greek word *canon,* meaning "measuring rule," was used to refer to these emerging standards for the church.

Constantine. Born about A.D. 280; died 337. His reign as Roman emperor began in 306 and lasted until his death. After a period during which the emperors had persecuted the Christians, Constantine determined to side with the Christians as a way of regaining strength and unity for Rome. Some historians think his espousal of Christianity was cynical and opportunist; others regard his conversion and efforts in behalf of Christianity as genuine.

deacon. From a Greek word for one who performs services for others. It came to be applied to those persons assigned modest responsibilities in the early Christian communities.

Dead Sea community, Dead Sea Scrolls. The Jewish religious sect that occupied the site of a complex of buildings resembling a monastery on a bluff overlooking the Dead Sea from the northwest. During excavations in the 1950s, scrolls were found stored in caves in the area. These original documents provide information about the rules of the community, their origin under a Teacher of Righteousness, their interpretations of scripture, and their expectations that God was going to enable them to purify the Temple in Jerusalem and establish what they considered to be the pure worship of the God of Israel there. The group is probably identical with the Essenes, whose existence and some of whose teachings are known from first century A.D. Jewish sources (Josephus and Philo).

Elijah. A prophet of the ninth century B.C., whose acts and words are reported in I Kings 17–II Kings 2. His courage in denouncing the idolatrous practices of the kings of Israel and Judah and his mysterious departure to heaven (II Kings 2) led later prophets to predict that God would bring him back to earth to prepare Israel for the final judgment (Malachi 4:5–6). Early Christian tradition identified John the Baptist with Elijah (Matthew 17:10–13).

Enoch. A mysterious figure described briefly in Genesis 5:18–24, who, like Elijah, did not depart this life through death, but "walked with God." His return was likewise awaited by certain pious Jews, and a group of writings purporting to have been written by him were widely used by Jews (including the Dead Sea community) and by early Christians. See Jude 14, which quotes from the Book of Enoch.

Ephesians. A letter which claims to have been written by Paul, but which on the grounds of style and content is more probably written by a later admirer of Paul. Imitating the apostle's style, the author stresses the need for unity of faith and practice in the church. Ephesus, one of the chief cities of Asia Minor, was visited by Paul and became a major Christian center.

Epictetus. Born in Phrygia (in what is now Turkey) about A.D. 60, he was brought to Rome as a slave, but obtained his freedom there and became a leading Stoic philosopher. His life was characterized by perseverance, contentment, and courage in the face of adversity. The summary of his teachings is preserved in a handbook known as the *Enchiridion.*

Eucharist. From a Greek word meaning "giving of thanks." The term is applied to the ritual meal which developed in the early church on the basis of the tradition of Jesus' last supper with his disciples on the eve of his crucifixion. He is reported to have used the occasion of the meal to remind them of their common commitment to the work of preparing for God's kingdom ("This is the New Covenant"), of the perception that in some way his impending death ratified the New Covenant ("my body . . . my blood . . . for you"), and of the coming era when they would be reunited and vindicated by God ("until I drink it in the kingdom of God"). Modeled in part on the Dead Sea meal of unity and future fulfillment, it came to be regarded as a continual sacrifice through which the faithful were able to gain forgiveness of their sins—that is, the Mass.

Eusebius. A Christian scholar from Caesarea in Palestine, who became court advisor to the emperor Constantine. He is the author of the great *Ecclesiastical History,* which not only traced the development of the church down to the fourth century, but also incorporated quotations from scores of ancient documents and writers that might otherwise have been lost to posterity.

Gnosticism. A view of the world that regards existence as a cosmic conflict between good (spirit) and evil (matter). Human beings are believed to be basically spiritual, children of light, but they have become trapped in the dark world of matter. A redeemer from the realm of spirit has come to free them. Knowledge (in Greek, *gnosis*) of this process and of the heavenly spheres through which the redeemed may pass on their way back to the realm of light has been granted only to those initiated into the circle of the "knowers" (the gnostics). Some scholars think this world view antedated Christianity, while others consider it to have been an outgrowth of Christianity which drew heavily on Jewish speculation about Wisdom as agent of God in creating and redeeming the world. A library of Gnostic writings was discovered in Upper Egypt in 1945, greatly increasing knowledge of this movement, which was otherwise known almost solely from attacks made on it by Christian opponents.

gospel. From an old English word that means the same as the Greek term it translates *(evangelion):* "good news." It is used in the Old Testament in connection with the prophetic predictions of God's redemptive purpose for His people (for example, Isaiah 61:1), and was the basic term used to describe Jesus' announcement and actions to prepare his hearers for the coming of God's rule (Mark 1:1, 15; Luke 4:16–21). Perhaps because Mark used it in the opening words of his report of Jesus, it came to be the term for all the narratives about Jesus and his teachings. As a literary form, the gospel is a unique Christian creation.

hedonism. A view of life which regards pleasure as the highest good.

Isis. Egyptian goddess, wife of Osiris, who played an important role in the mythology of Greek and Roman times, serving as the one who delivered Osiris from his enemies and thus restored the fertility of the Nile, and as the instrument of Wisdom through whom the world was created and is sustained. Shrines of Isis have been found from Syria to Spain on both sides of the Mediterranean.

Islam. The religious movement launched by Muhammad, a prophet from central Arabia, who beginning in 622 called his people to a life of purity and discipline in obedience to the one God, Allah. Muhammad recognized as prophetic predecessors many of the figures of the Old Testament (Moses, Abraham, Solomon), and set down in the Qur'an (or Koran) the revelations made to him by Allah. The holy city for those who follow his call to submission to God is Mecca, to which Muslims are expected to make pilgrimages. (For details, see the book titled *Islam* in this series.)

Knox, John. One of the leaders of the Protestant Reformation in Scotland (1505–1572). The Church of Scotland developed a structure of leadership through elected representatives, called elders or (from the Greek term) presbyters. From this came the name and organizational pattern of the Presbyterian churches.

Law of Moses. The body of regulations recorded in the Old Testament books of Genesis, Exodus, Leviticus, Numbers, and Deuteronomy. In their present form, these laws developed over a period of centuries (from the twelfth to at least the sixth centuries B.C.), but all came to be attributed to Moses. Later Jewish tradition taught that the authority of Moses was also transmitted to the official intrepreters of his law, so that the term can be used for (1) the legal material in the Bible attributed to Moses, (2) the first five books of the Old Testament, also called the Pentateuch, or Torah, and (3) the official Jewish legal tradition.

Lombards. A Germanic people who invaded northern Italy and established a kingdom there in the sixth century A.D.

Maccabean. The nickname given to Judah (Judas), the leader of the Jewish revolt against the Seleucid kings who ruled Palestine from Antioch in the early second century B.C. Two historical accounts of the exploits of this Jewish liberation movement are included in the Roman Catholic Bible (First and Second Maccabees); other books of Maccabees offer valuable insights as to how deeply the Jews of this period were influenced by Greek-style culture even as they were freeing themselves from Greek political domination.

Mount Athos. A mountainous peninsula in northern Greece, projecting into the Aegean Sea; the location of many large monasteries and of hundreds of caves and structures where orthodox monks have lived over the past fifteen hundred years.

Neoplatonism. A philosophical movement of the third century A.D. that sought to revive the essence of the idealistic philosophy of Plato (see *Plato*), but to combine it with elements of mysticism. The result was a religious philosophy which was critical of Christianity but which strongly influenced Christian thought, especially that of Origen of Alexandria and Augustine of Hippo.

Nero. Roman emperor from A.D. 54 to 68. Erratic and extravagant, he tried to blame the Christians for the consequences of some of his unpopular acts and martyred many Christians in Rome.

Nestorius. Patriarch of Constantinople in the fifth century. His view that Christ had two distinct natures—human and divine—became dominant in the churches of eastern Syria, Iraq, and Iran. Later, Nestorianism spread eastward across central Asia to Tibet and China, but it was repressed in the Middle East by the rise of Islam.

Ninian. One of a group of church leaders who came from the mainland of Europe to the British Isles to carry out the evangelization of those lands in the fifth and sixth centuries.

oracle. A sacred place where a god communicates information to the faithful, as at Delphi, the shrine of Apollo in central Greece. The message was conveyed through a priest or priestess.

Patrick. As a youth, Patrick was carried off from Britain to slavery in Ireland. After about six years he escaped, probably to France. Early in the fifth century he returned to Ireland in the successful attempt to convert its inhabitants to Christianity.

Peter the Hermit. From Amiens in France, Peter preached in behalf of the First Crusade (in the later eleventh century) and helped lead it.

Plato(nism). The dominant philosophy of idealism. Building on the tradition of Socrates (470?–399 B.C.), Plato (427?–347 B.C.) developed a view of reality which regarded all earthly objects and experiences as imperfect, decaying copies of eternal archetypes. The moral life could be achieved only by shaping one's life in accord with the ideals of truth and justice.

Pliny the Younger. Nephew and adopted son of Pliny the Elder, author of an encyclopedic *Natural History*. Born in A.D. 61, during the reign of Nero, he rose quickly in the government. At age forty-two he was appointed by Trajan as governor of Bithynia, a province in eastern Asia Minor (Turkey) threatened with invasion from the east by the Parthians. His correspondence with Trajan has been preserved, including a famous letter in which he asks how to treat the Christians who were a rapidly multiplying sect in his province.

Pontius Pilate. Procurator (governor) of Judea from A.D. 26 to 36 under appointment of the emperor Tiberius, after the descendants of Herod had proved incapable of ruling this politically explosive region. Pilate's vacillation between weakness and ruthlessness led to his dismissal.

presbytery. Council of the elders (in Greek, *presbyterio*), the major decision-making group within the early congregations of Christians.

relics. Bones, hair, clothing, or other remains of the saints of the church. The objects came to be venerated as sacred and were believed to convey certain powers of healing or other spiritual benefits.

revival(ist). A type of movement that has occurred at various times in the history of the church, characterized by stress on the need for repentance, on individual conversion and commitment, and on emotional or ecstatic evidence of faith. Some free church groups even today have annual revival meetings, in which the Spirit is believed to be manifest in dramatic ways in order to renew the members in the faith.

Samaria. A region in central Palestine which was the center for the northern tribes of Israel after the reign of Solomon (eleventh century B.C.) and the splitting up of the kingdom. A central shrine was erected at Samaria in competition with the Jerusalem Temple, and a somewhat different version of the Law of Moses developed. A tiny sect of Samaritans continues that tradition today, with its own priesthood, shrine, rites, and sacred writings.

scripture. A word, meaning "writing," used to refer to the sacred, authoritative writings of Judaism or of Christianity. In the New Testament, the Christian claim that Jesus is the fulfillment of the promises made by God to ancient Israel is documented by appeal to the scriptures, as in Luke 4:16–21 or Romans 1:1–4.

Stoicism. A philosophical tradition which stressed that the universe was ordered by natural law, and that human beings could find peace and happiness only by harmonizing their lives with the laws of nature.

Titus. Roman emperor from A.D. 79 to 81. Son of Vespasian, he led the Roman forces that stormed Jerusalem in A.D. 70, sacking the city and destroying its great Temple.

Vespasian. Roman emperor from A.D. 69 to 79. Placed in charge of the troops by Nero to quell the Jewish revolt of 66–71, Vespasian was acclaimed emperor by his army after the struggle for power that occurred at the death of Nero. He and Titus shared in the triumph—and the treasure— that followed the fall of Jerusalem in A.D. 70.

Zoroastrianism. A religious teacher who lived around 600 B.C. is credited with this system of beliefs, which perceives the universe as a cosmic conflict between Ahura-mazda (the good god of light) and Ahriman (the evil god of darkness). The former is aided by angels, the latter by demons. By performing certain rituals and by practicing ascetic ways of life, it is possible to gain freedom from the power of darkness and achieve redemption in the realm of light. These ideas, which probably influenced Judaism and early Christianity, flourished across the Middle East until the rise of Islam in the seventh century A.D.

Suggestions for Further Reading

On the rise of Christianity in the New Testament period:
Kee, Howard C., Young, F. W., and Froehlich, K. *Understanding the New Testament.* 3d ed. Englewood Cliffs, N.J.: Prentice-Hall, 1973.

On Jesus and the gospels:
Kee, Howard C. *Jesus in History: An Approach to the Study of the Gospels.* 2d ed. New York: Harcourt Brace Jovanovich, 1977. (paperback)

Documents and primary sources for the history of Christianity:
Kee, Howard C. *The Origins of Christianity: Sources and Documents.* Englewood Cliffs, N.J.: Prentice-Hall, 1973. (paperback)
Petry, Ray, and Manschreck, Clyde, eds. *A History of Christianity.* 2 vols. Englewood Cliffs, N.J.: Prentice-Hall, 1964.

On the history of the early church:
Chadwick, Henry. *The Early Church. Pelican History of the Church,* Vol. 1. New York: Penguin Books, 1968. (paperback)

On the church in later periods:
Ahlstrom, Sidney E. *Religious History of the American People.* 2 vols. New York: Doubleday & Co., 1975. (paperback)
Atiya, Aziz S. *History of Eastern Christianity.* Notre Dame, Ind.: University of Notre Dame Press, 1968.
Cherry, C. Conrad. *God's New Israel: Religious Interpretations of American Destiny.* Englewood Cliffs, N.J.: Prentice-Hall, 1971. (paperback)
Dillenberger, John, and Welch, Claude. *Protestant Christianity: Interpreted Through Its Development.* New York: Charles Scribners' Sons, 1954. (paperback)
McKenzie, John L. *The Roman Catholic Church.* New York: Doubleday & Co., 1971. (paperback)

On the conflict of religion and reason:
Baumer, Franklin L. *Religion and the Rise of Scepticism.* New York: Harcourt Brace Jovanovich, 1969. (paperback)

DATE DUE